IMAGES OF LONDON

ABOUT
WILLESDEN
AND WEMBLEY

LEN SNOW

The History Press

Acknowledgements

I am indebted as always to the Brent Local History Archives for allowing the use of their vast store of images and especially for the whole-hearted support, experience and knowledge of their brilliant Archivist, Tina Morton, and her staff. All photographs not otherwise indicated are drawn from the Archive and printed with their consent.

Information and photographs from the current president of Collingham Cricket Club, Mr G.T. Woodcock; and from Nottinghamshire and Lincolnshire Library Service.

With appreciation to: Staples Mattress Co.; Geoff Hewlett's *History of Kenton*; National Portrait Gallery; BAe; National Railway Museum; London Transport Museum; M.G. Thomas; Granada Television; BBC; Guinness; John Barrells's *The dark side of the landscape*; the brilliant monograph, the 'Jubilee History of the Willesden Library Service', published in 1954; Martin Curley's article in the *Wembley History Society Journal*; article on J.L. Baird in *Jones Telecommunications and Multimedia Encyclopedia*;Victor Silvester's biography; the Peter Wilkinson website and to Terry Lomas, Dick Weindling and Marianne Colloms, authors of *Kilburn and West Hampstead Past*, Phillimore & Co. 1999; Bob Langford, Cemeteries Director and Shaun Faulkner, Parks Manager for Brent; *Notes by A.S. Travis, on William Perkin,* 1983; The Journals of the Royal Agricultural Society; the head teacher of Oliver Goldsmith Primary School, Brent;the head teacher of John Kelly Technology College.

My heartfelt thanks, as ever, to my dearest wife, proof-reader *extraordinaire,* supporter and (hardly-ever) complainant of the time I take to write these histories.

First published 2007
Reprinted 2008, 2014

The History Press
The Mill, Brimscombe Port,
Stroud, Gloucestershire, GL5 2QG
www.thehistorypress.co.uk

British Library Cataloguing in Publication Data.
A catalogue record for this book is available from the British Library.

ISBN 978 0 7524 4297 6

Printed and bound in Great Britain by
Marston Book Services Limited, Oxfordshire

ABOUT
WILLESDEN
AND WEMBLEY

It is my pleasure to congratulate
you on achieving 25 years
service to Local Government

Contents

Introduction

One Thousand Years of Brent

A bit naughtily, I start the Millennium history 1,000 years even earlier! This enables me to pick up in the year 50AD when the Romans had just about completed some of their first roads, including Dover to London and from London to Wroxeter, near Shrewsbury. This is the one later called Watling Street, which is now Kilburn High Road and Cricklewood Broadway – the eastern boundary of Willesden for 1,000 years and more. It was a major traffic artery for the Romans, and is still, after almost 2,000 years.

The Romans colonised England until 410AD and after they left the so-called Dark Ages set in; the Anglo-Saxons gradually settling in and taking over. The territory of Brent (taking its name from the British word for the little river which flows through its centre) became home to a few small tribes whose names live on in the villages which grew out of their farms: Toca in Tokyngton, Wemba in Wembley, Herewulf in Harlesden, and Alprecht in Alperton (sometimes called Appletown!). In some cases, the lie of the land contributed to the naming of areas: Neasden, the nose-shaped hill; Kilburn, the kyle (or cow)-stream; Willesden, the hill of the spring.

At the end of the tenth century, the worshippers at the three churches (if they then existed) at St Mary's on Harrow Hill, at old St Andrews, Kingsbury and St Mary's Willesden might have learned, with terror and also excitement, of the coming of the second Millennium since Christ was born. Their simple lives centred round the land they tilled and the church. Some would take an interest in local affairs through the *Moot* (or Hundred) at the Gore (so-named because the shape of the field of the meeting-place was like a gore of cloth – the site commemorated by a carving on the wall of the Police Station at Kingsbury) or the Ossulstone Hundred.

The Norman Conquest may have shaken the state of England, but it probably caused little change in the sedate mode of life in this quiet countryside, barely ten miles from the capital, London. Soon the King's Commissioners would be coming round to collect information for the Domesday Book which was completed in 1087. We learn that Canterbury 'holds' Harrow, which then included Wembley; St Paul's held Willesden and Harlesden; and St Peter's (Westminster) had control over Kingsbury. These church links continued for many centuries, but most farms were leased out and sub-let. Other lands were acquired by different landowners; for example All Souls College had land gifted by their benefactor, Archbishop Chichele, and this included some in Kingsbury, in Cricklewood (where the sale of timber from the woods was dutifully noted in 1597 and other years) and in Harlesden.

John Lyon had a large farm at Preston and was rich enough to help found and endow Harrow School ('for the poor sons of local farmers') and to leave a bequest which still benefits the repair of local roads. At Uxendon Manor, in the reign of Elizabeth I, the Bellamy family, headed by the indomitable Kathleen, was persecuted for harbouring Catholic priests and also the wretched Anthony Babington, who plotted to kill the Queen and replace her with Mary Queen of Scots.

During the Civil War, it is possible to imagine the Cromwellian, Sir William Roberts, Lord of the Manor of Neasden, glowering from Dollis Hill at Royalist Richard Page who had taken over Uxendon at Barn Hill. Roberts' influence with Cromwell may well have protected St Mary's church in Willesden in the Civil War.

Despite the ravages of the Black Death in 1349 (Kingsbury village lost about half its population), the effects of the Civil War and the hardships caused by the Napoleonic War, Brent hardly changed much over the first 800 years of this Millennium. The countryside was a rural backwater; the farms were managed by a succession of landowners, many of whom were absent and relied on bailiffs. Enclosures of fields was rare until the beginning of the nineteenth century – this brought about the familiar patchwork of fields with their hedges and fences. Here came, in the 1770s, the famous author Oliver Goldsmith; he lived in Shell Cottage on Kingsbury Road. Another great writer, Harrison Ainsworth, came to the quiet Brondesbury district in the 1830s, living at The Elms on Kilburn High Road.

In 1822, a magazine had an article about Willesden village describing 'an elegant seat' (Brondesbury Manor House) opposite 'an antique farmhouse', the village 'with the appearance of a sequestered spot. On the right is Dollar's Hill [sic]…'!

And then … the new industrial world came to Brent. In 1801 the canal cut its way across Alperton and Harlesden, part of the waterway which joined London and Birmingham. The delightful inn, the Grand Junction Arms on Acton Lane, is a pleasing reminder of the past glories of water-borne traffic. However, the canals were soon over-shadowed by the new railways. In 1837, the world's first main-line route was built by George Stephenson (& Son) from London to Birmingham (almost paralleling the canal) – passing through Kilburn, Harlesden, Wembley and Kenton – changing the face of Brent for ever.

Its impact was slow to realise, but by the 1860s Kilburn was beginning to be built up as an extension of London, and Harlesden village had started to grow. Soon the area was criss-crossed with railway lines was and the commuter age was born. With the installation of pure piped drinking water and then main drainage sewers, the way was open for Willesden (and later Wembley and Kingsbury) to come into full existence as the new suburbia.

In Wembley, meanwhile, the still-rural village benefited from the philanthropy of the Copland sisters who, among other contributions to their adopted home, built St Johns Church and caused Wembley parish to be created. Their home was later acquired by the Barham family, who had founded the Express Dairy Co. – thus adding two illustrious names to the local scene, commemorated in many ways, including a school named after each family.

Willesden continued to expand from its early development in South Kilburn so quickly that in the 1890s it was the fastest growing district in London (as was Wembley in the 1920s and Kingsbury in the 1930s).

So rapid was this that it inspired Gus Elen's song: 'By climbing up the chimbley/You can see across to Wembley,/If it wasn't for the 'ouses in between'.

Willesden acquired the first trappings of local democracy in 1875 with its Local Board (public health for Wembley was still controlled from Harrow). In 1895, Willesden and Wembley (which for a few years incorporated Kingsbury) each became District Councils.

Even with this rapid build-up of houses, and some factories, Willesden was still rural enough in 1879 to be able to stage the Royal Agricultural Show, on 60 acres of land in Kilburn. Some of this was later protected as Queen's Park, but the rest fell under the developers' bricks-and-mortar onslaught.

Schools were built, starting with St Mary's (near the church in Willesden), Princess Frederica and Alperton; new churches catered for the growing population – Christchurch in Brondesbury, All Soul's in Harlesden, as well as Catholic churches, returning after 350 years and non-denominational chapels and churches. Railways extended – the Metropolitan to Harrow and later the District (now Piccadilly) through Alperton and Sudbury.

With the arrival of the last century of the Millennium, the pace of change quickened even more. As Willesden grew, it took control of its elementary education. Kingsbury became a District Council in its own right (until, frightened by expanding Willesden in 1930, it jumped back into the arms of Wembley). As housing estates sprang up, efforts were made to protect the green open spaces ('the lungs') that had been farms and woodlands – thus Roundwood Park and Gladstone Park were acquired by a far-seeing Council.

After the Great War, the British Empire Exhibition at Wembley and Wembley Stadium (redeveloped as the new National Stadium) gave a great impetus to the opening up of the area, and 'Metroland' was borne. We nearly had an Eiffel Tower of our own, but Watkin's Folly (later the site of the Stadium) failed to survive. As John Betjeman wrote: 'When melancholy Autumn comes to Wembley/And electric trains are lighted after tea/The Poplars near the Stadium are trembly/With their tap and tap and whispering to me'.

In the 1930s Kingsbury acquired its sister Queensbury and yet more pleasant countryside near London was covered in road after road of delightful 'semis' as 'homes for heroes' became the new suburbia. Here, John Logie Baird took over a charming mansion in Roe Green Park for some of his first television experiments. In Wembley, firms like Laing, Comben & Wakeling and Callow & Wright built large, planned estates on the rolling farms that once provided hay for London's myriad horses. In Willesden, by the 1930's, many of the original houses built in Kilburn for the workers had become slums and a clearance programme was the urgent concern of the new Labour Council.

Up on Dollis Hill, the Post Office Research Station made a striking addition to the Neasden skyline (as the building still does, though no longer used for its original purpose). Nearby, at Tankridge Close the first tanks of the First World War were tested. Guinness built an equally dominant and well-designed brewery at Park Royal (now, infuriatingly destroyed) and the Gaumont State Cinema at Kilburn with its glittering foyer was, in 1937, the largest cinema in Europe.

Willesden, and later Kingsbury and Wembley, became highly industrialised, particularly during and after the First World War. Kingsbury developed as a major airplane centre and Park Royal (partly in Ealing) also became involved in armaments. Post-war the units were converted for industrial and commercial uses. As the North Circular Road was built as a major new artery, it became the centre of many new industries including Smith's Crisps (Smith's clocks was nearby) and Staples Furniture (hence 'Staple's Corner', although that firm has now moved away). The site of the British Empire Exhibition became the Wembley Trading Estate.

After the Second World War, Willesden, Labour controlled since 1933, and Wembley set about dealing with war damage and providing homes for their growing population - and for many who flocked to London in search of work – from Wales, Scotland, Ireland and other parts of England. The area has always been attractive – apart from the Anglo-Saxons and Normans at the beginning of this Millennium, there have been Irish farm-workers, recruited to work on the canals ('navvies' – navigational canal workers), Jewish refugees from Russia and then from Nazi oppression. In 1964, Willesden and Wembley were reluctantly merged to form the London Borough of Brent. More recently, those from the New Commonwealth – West Indies, India, Bangladesh – and many more: all absorbed into the rich mixture which has become Brent today.

one

Makers of Brent

The Man who Built my Road

When I give one of my talks on local history, I usually begin by explaining my curiosity to find the origin of the name of my road – Norton Road. Who, or what, was Norton? It was not very difficult – it turned out that it, and its neighbours, were villages in Lincolnshire, near the town of Newark (which is actually in Nottinghamshire).

My interest was stirred. How did this link between Lincoln and Wembley come about? Who was behind it? When did it happen? It was becoming a bit like a detective story. I quickly learned that the person concerned was named Curtis and he was living in the village of South Collingham (which is on the border of Nottinghamshire and Lincolnshire) in the 1890s when he decided to invest money in buying land in Wembley, of all places.

Wembley had been growing, slowly, during the last quarter of Victoria's reign, especially around the High Road and the station (then called Sudbury for Wembley). One by one, farms were surrendered for housing developments. One of these was to the east of Sudbury Park Farm, the model dairy farm run by Titus Barham, between Chaplin Road and the Ealing Road, and this was the area bought by Mr Curtis.

I had to find out more about Curtis. My wife and I visited South Collingham and found a lot of information by talking to the local librarian and the estate agent – whose firm just happened to be the very same which Curtis had consulted a hundred years earlier. It was called Smith Woolley.

I obtained from the office of George Ward, estate agents in Wembley High Road for most of the last century, some plans of the sale of land from the Curtis Estate. In the 1890s, Curtis was looking for more land in which to invest and he turned for advice to his cousin, who was a partner in the firm of Smith Woolley. They, in turn, used their family connection to identify this area of Wembley. Charles Dalton Woolley, a solicitor was living at High Lea (now the site of the Park Lane Methodist church), and his stockbroker cousin John Turton Woolley (Turton Road, off Lancelot Road in Wembley is named for him) was at Wembley House – before it was acquired by Col. Topham (it is now the site of Copland School).

In 1873, J.T. Woolley had acquired from Mrs Sarah Hurcomb the land between Watery Lane (as Ealing Road used to be called) and Chaplin Road (though it did not then bear that name – that came from a Government Minister of the late nineteenth century, Henry Chaplin). Woolley then sold on the estate to Curtis – the land where I and my wife – and hundreds of others – now live.

In the next ten years or so, into the Edwardian years of the twentieth century, the local firm of George Ward set up development plans, tying in with the local council's own Town Planning scheme. The roads were sketched out on the map. Curiously, the name of Curtis' own village of Collingham was not used. One, Aubourn, was originally put in, but never built on – saving some of the open space for One Tree Hill. Most of the rest were actually the Lincolnshire villages where the Curtis family owned their land – Eagle, Norton Disney, Bassingham, Swinderby, where Charles was lord of the manor (it now houses an RAF station), Scarle and four or five others on the estate. (Holland Road is named after a local builder, even though it sounds as if it also has a Lincolnshire connection). Builders bought into the plots – which explains the variety of house styles in these roads. Curtis employed, as architects, his local firm of Smith, Woolley and local builders came in to do the work – Scull, Comben & Wakeling, Meecoms and others.

Among the first to be built, in the early 1900s, were some charming 'villas' at 102-112 Ealing Road, many of which are still in use today, complete, in most cases with their simple pargetting on the cornices. The other roads were laid out according to the master plan, with some slight

Signpost in Lincolnshire linking Curtis' home with his Wembley development.

Memorial plaque to Charles Constable Curtis in South Collingham church.

10

variants as the development proceeded. Comben & Wakeling produced a brochure of their 'charming and artistic villas in Beautiful, Healthy Wembley' for as little as £400. One of the attractions mentioned was J. Sainsbury's shop which then – and for about fifty more years – was open at the corner of the Harrow (or High) Road and Ealing Road.

Most of the roads on the Curtis Estate were partly built on by 1914. A larger number of houses were erected as part of the huge expansion of Wembley in the 1920s, generated by the Wembley Exhibition. Some more – like my own – were the product of further expansion in the thirties. The estate was a good, though typical, example of suburbia – tree-lined, semi-detached (for the most part), friendly and neighbourly.

In continuing my saga in search of Curtis, I wrote to the local newspaper in Newark and this produced an amazing result. A local resident, Mr Trevor Woodcock, replied and we started up a delightful correspondence. He had been born in Collingham in 1932 – had now become the president of the Collingham cricket club, as had Curtis before him. He knew Charles' son, Major Lancelot Curtis – also a president of the cricket club. Trevor gave me a great deal of background to the Curtis family and their connection with Collingham and the district around, which I have used in this article. One little story he told me is a lovely illustration of life as it was:

One Saturday morning I was talking to an old Collingham resident when he told me that it was his job to carry chairs from South Collingham House to the cricket ground on Saturday morning. He said he was the garden boy there and the chairs came from the house because the Curtis family lived there. I then asked him when that would be; he thought for a while and then said it would be before the war. I said you mean the 1914-18 war and he said oh no, the Boer War. Imagine in 1970 someone referring to the Boer War as 'The War'!

Charles Constable Curtis – to give him his full name – was born in Berkhamsted in 1852, the eldest son of Captain Constable Curtis. The Curtis family fortune was, reputedly, made by Tom Curtis who, just before the Crimean War, bought up a lot of gunpowder, which he then sold to the government. The family then invested their money in land – much of it around Collingham and Swinderby and other farms in the nearby villages – just those whose names appear on the roads in Wembley. Tom Curtis also seems to have bought the Dairy Farm, to the east of Wembley Green, and when the estate was itself developed in the early twentieth century, the roads came from his area, Berkhamsted – of course – and Tring, Aldbury, Flamstead and others.

Charles had several brothers and sisters, with whom he remained in touch throughout his life. He married Edith Onslow, the daughter of the rector of Catmore in Berkshire, who lived at Benham Cottage near Newbury, and the newly-wed couple came to live in South Collingham House, in the district to which they remained faithful for the rest of their long lives. He soon joined in public life, becoming the epitome of the country squire. He was appointed to the magistrate's bench in 1889 and was made Deputy Lieutenant (the Queen's representative for the county). Among so many opportunities to serve the community, just a few more may be mentioned. He became chairman of the Quarter Sessions and of the Newark bench of magistrates (until his death). I am delighted, though not surprised, to learn that he became chairman of the Newark Rural District Council. He was also – and he very much threw himself into this – the president of Newark Hospital. What he did for his adopted village of Collingham was legendary – president of the cricket club was just one of many. Although he moved down the road to Langford Hall, he remained the local squire. Rather sadly, it seems he never received any public honour such as an OBE – though I can well believe that he never sought such recognition, being content that the appreciation of his friends and his community was enough reward. His son, Lance, lived in Mayfield House in South Collingham, now a nursing home.

Norton Road, Wembley – an early Curtis development, still there today though with modern window frames!

He died in 1936 very much honoured, loved and appreciated. He had a great send off as the report of his funeral shows, with mourners from both the Curtis and Woolley families and notables such as the Earl and Countess of Liverpool, Lord Charles Cavendish-Bentinck and the Bishop of Southwell. He is buried – as his memorial shows – with other members of his family in All Saints, Collingham. He was very much the country gentleman – yet he created a suburban estate in London. I was pleased when Brent Council agreed to my suggestion to name a road in his memory – Curtis Lane – the man who built my road.

The Man Who Built Watkin's Folly

Although he did not invent the word, it was Edward Watkin who laid the foundations for the exquisitely named area of London's suburbia – 'Metroland' – but he is, quite unfairly but inescapably, linked to his one mistake – 'Watkin's Folly'.

Edward William Watkin became one of the greatest of the 'Railway Kings' – the handful of entrepreneurs who saw the opportunities in developing rail travel and took the risks needed to achieve their ambitions. His greatest idea – unrealised in his lifetime – was to be able to travel by train from Manchester to Paris, through a Channel Tunnel…!! – and that was his one unachieved project (it took Margaret Thatcher to complete that for him).

He was born in Manchester in 1819, where his father owned a cotton mill. He joined the family business after his schooling finished but also interested himself in his local community – he started a Saturday half-day movement and raised money to open public parks – which was later carried over into the creation of Wembley Park. By the time he was twenty he was involved in one of the big political campaigns of the day – the Anti-Corn Law League, which brought him into contact with

Above left: Sir Edward Watkin, railway king, creator of Wembley Park and builder of Watkin's Folly. (Courtesy of National Railway Museum)

Above right: Watkin's Folly – correctly the Wembley Tower, the intended London rival to the Paris Eiffel Tower, looking desolate shortly before demolition in 1907.

the political world which was to play a large part in his life. In 1845 he took up his first post in the occupation that became his life's work - he became secretary of the Trent Valley Railway Company (and married his sweetheart, Mary). Soon after, that company was taken over by the thrusting new London and North Western Railway (which had started as the London and Birmingham in 1837, the first mainline trunk railway – see p.25). There he came under the tutelage of the masterful Mark Huish, the General Manager, who happened to live in Harlesden House.

Eight years later, he became general manager of the company which was to become the mainstay of his career – the Manchester, Sheffield and Lincolnshire (MSL, which later, in his final years, he expanded into the Great Central with its London terminus at Marylebone and was present at its opening in a wheelchair). Within ten years he was chairman and stayed for thirty more.

He became an MP (for Stockport and later for Hythe) – off and on – as a Liberal, though with a strongly independent approach to many issues of the day. He acquired chairmanships of railway companies as if he was playing a game of Monopoly – how he found time for all this, only another busy person would understand. He was, we would say today, a 'workaholic'. He was knighted in 1868 and made a Baronet in 1880.

His renown in the railway world led to invitations to help other countries' problems. He went to Canada and created the Canadian National Railway – and had a hand in the creation of the Canadian Confederation in 1867. He also helped in Greece and in India. For his work both on the English railways and internationally he was highly praised by William Gladstone.

To further his vision of the Manchester to Paris operation, he became involved with the Channel Tunnel Company, the South Eastern Railway and the Metropolitan – becoming chairman of them too. His frustration showed when, excellent companies as all these were, he failed to gain control of any of the major railway lines into London. So, he built his own – the Great Central!

Of all of these, the Metropolitan was to prove his biggest triumph – and involve him in his biggest disaster. The Met had been started, in 1863 (it had been the inspiration of Charles Pearson), and ran from Paddington to Farringdon, under Euston Road for the most part. It was the first underground railway in the world. It was then extended, in stages, east and west. A separate development was a line from Baker Street to Swiss Cottage in 1868, which was incorporated in the Metropolitan Extension which reached out to Harrow in 1879 and 1880. There was a board room revolution in the Metropolitan Company in 1872 which brought in the highly experienced Watkin. His skill brought warring factions together and enabled them to work towards the expansion. This eventually allowed passengers to travel from Baker Street through Willesden, Wembley and Harrow out to Verney Junction and Brill in the heart of the Buckinghamshire countryside enabling a link-up with his beloved MSL.

Building the railway involved buying the land and among the acres which were acquired was an estate called Wembley Park sometimes known as the White House from its mansion. It is today identified by roads like Manor Drive and Wembley Park Drive and the partly-preserved thatched lodge at the junction with Wembley Hill Road. Watkin visualised an amusement park on some of this land and this his company duly created with a lake, cricket, running track, trotting and, later, a golf course all served by their specially built station with the same name - now very recently spectacularly rebuilt to serve the equally spectacular new stadium. A large swathe of land was still available and this became the heart of the suburban development that the Metropolitan Railway Company envisaged as boosting their passenger traffic – in 1916 one of its staff named the concept 'Metroland' and, hymned by John Betjeman, that is where many of the readers of this book now live.

Watkin then planned the final glory, to make his dream come pertially true - a tower, like the Eiffel tower in Paris, linking London and Paris symbolically. A competition was held and the winning design. unsurprisingly, was very like the Paris original. Building started in 1894 on that part of Wembley Park which was later to be Wembley Stadium. A year later it had reached 155ft above the ground and was opened to the public as a first instalment. Sad to tell, it did not become a popular attraction, unlike the rest of Wembey Park; money ran out to continue building and the decision was taken to dismantle it. In May 1907, with Watkin dead six years (he did not live to see one major failure) it was blown up. Alas, 'Watkin's Folly' is all that remains of his one-time fame,

George Furness – Chief Engineer

If you take a walk along the Victoria Embankment from Westminster Bridge eastwards, you may be forgiven for not realising that history is not only all around you but also beneath your feet. Below the roadway is the Circle Line (originally part of the Metropolitan Railway) and below that is one of London's main sewers – part of the network that serves the Metropolis. The engineer of the Metropolitan Board of Works, Sir Joseph Bazalgette, designed the grand scheme.

Between 1864 and 1870 a large part of the enormous task of constructing the sewer and the road above was carried out by one of the best-known contractors of the day – George Furness. He was born in the village of Longstone in Derbyshire on 21 October 1820 – hence Longstone Avenue which runs alongside Roundwood Park which became his Willesden home.

He began working in railway contracting – this was the period of the Railway Mania – and gradually built up a large business of his own – becoming famous in the civil engineering world for the contracts he undertook. He began in the Midlands, near the area where he was born, but soon expanded into railway contracts all over the Midlands and also in France. Here he worked

Above: Roundwood House, Harlesden – home to the Furness family from 1856 to 1936.

Right: George Furness, when this civil engineer was elected to become the first chairman of the Willesden Local Board, *c.* 1875.

with one of the other great contractors – Thomas Brassey – and they became good friends as well as business partners.

He built the mainline railway in Brazil. He became wealthy. Among the biggest of his overseas works was at Odessa, after the Crimean War (1854-6), when the Russians called him in to restore public works damaged in that fighting. Bazalgette and another well-known engineer, John Rennie, helped him in getting the contract – and this connection may have helped him obtain the Embankment work.

He also undertook work on dredging in Italy – Palermo, Spezia, Leghorn and Ancona – and all the towns mentioned here were used to name roads in the vicinity of the main road that bears his own name in Harlesden.

Repeated plagues of cholera and the persistent and growing menace of sewage emptying into the Thames, culminating in the 'Great Stink' of 1858, created the demand for action. Spurred on by Sir Joseph Paxton MP (builder of the original Crystal Palace), Parliament agreed to the building of a huge main sewer next to the Thames in central London. Bazalgette issued contracts for the Embankment (this was the heart of the new scheme) to several major engineering firms: Furness was one of them and it was one of his biggest. There was some controversy about the awarding of that task – probably more to do with internal politics in the Board of Works than with the capability of Furness to do the job (although it nearly drove him bankrupt) – in fact it has lasted nearly one hundred and forty years already.

His success on this work crowned his career as a civil engineer and perhaps he now felt able to get married to a local girl, Sarah Rebecca Green from Ashford in Derbyshire, and this took place on 8 June 1864 – when he was no longer in the bloom of youth. However, he and his wife rapidly created a large family. This was not without tragedy. Three of the children died in infancy, but five survived. It was just as well George had bought a large house in Harlesden – Roundwood House, acquired in 1856. There were three girls and two boys. George John (the second so named, the first was one of those who died young) went to become an MP.

Meanwhile, Furness, who had settled into the role of local squire, was active in the affairs of the parish church, St Mary's and this led him more into the work of the community. On the commercial side, he built himself his own brick works at Chambers Lane, which had a chimney 145ft high, looming over Willesden Green belching out smoke across the town. It produced at least 120,000 bricks every three weeks and enabled him to supply not only his own building ventures in Cricklewood but many other sites. At one time he owned not only Roundwood House but also Grange Farm (where he created his brick works) and Church Farm on Church Road, Willesden.

He then took up with local politics and threw himself into the fight for Willesden's Right to Rule. Although he sided with the 'country' faction in opposing the demand for self-rule, against the urbanites of Kilburn, when the result was finally announced, he accepted the democratic result with good grace – so much so, that he was elected the first chairman of the new Willesden Local Board in 1875. He went on to become one of the first representatives on the Middlesex County Council, in 1888 – and, in that, was later followed by his son George John. He was involved with many other good works – the board of guardians and the school board, for example.

In public office, his tenacity of purpose, liberal views and ready regard for divergent opinions were well noted. He was an evangelical churchman and, in those days when the vestry was of real importance and meant hard fighting, he secured triumphant re-election year after year as the people's Churchwarden.

He was a tall man, described as 'a dear old country squire'; a generous and genial master to his workmen; a self-made man who conquered many obstacles and was left unspoilt by the wealth he attained. It is incredible to me that he received no public recognition not a knighthood, let

Above: The Willesden Local Board, resting after a meeting, at the Old Spotted Dog in Willesden Green High Road. In the centre of the front row is the chairman, F.A. Wood.

Right: The grand old man of Willesden, F.A. Wood, council leader and local historian.

Left: Leonard Chilcott, Brent Parks Manager, in one of his favourite gardens at Barham Park, 1972.

Opposite: Chilcott Nursery, opened by Brent Council and named in honour of their Parks Manager – visited in 1977 by the Mayor of Brent, Cllr George Swannell and his wife Mary (both on the right).

alone a baronetcy for his services to the country. When he died in January 1900, it was the end of an era in more ways than one.

There is the saddest of codicils to this history. One terrible tragedy preceded his death. His youngest daughter was murdered by her young husband, who then committed suicide. And after his death, his wife and two other children were drowned in a boating accident at Killarney Lakes. Mercifully, he was not there to bear the shock.

Creating Beauty

As Sir Christopher Wren said about his great work, St Paul's Cathedral, 'if you seek my monument, look around', so it can be said of Brent's former Parks Manager. As the *Wembley Observer* wrote, at the time of his retirement, 'no one can claim to have done more to create and preserve the beauty spots of Brent than Leonard Charles Chilcott'.

He was a quiet, modest gardener from Somerset, born in Bridgewater on 1 July 1908 – but that simple sentence belies the breadth of his contribution not just to Brent but to the world of horticulture. He started learning his trade at the age of fourteen in small private establishments before moving into local government in the parks section at Stalybridge in Cheshire. From there he gradually progressed in horticulture until his first senior appointment, in 1948 as Parks Manager in Wembley Borough Council.

The grounds of Barham Park, with its (then) lovely mansion, offered Chilcott his first challenge. Although the estate had been dedicated to the new borough by its intended Charter Mayor, George Titus Barham before his sudden death in 1937, the intervention of the war years from 1939 to 1945 had seen the park and the house being allowed to deteriorate. His efforts

there made Barham Park into one of the most attractively landscaped open spaces in Brent – although he had no say over the council's decision in 1957 to demolish the house.

He set up a new nursery there and this allowed him to grow flowers which were used at floral displays all over the borough and particularly at Mayoral Town Hall functions. The stage and front of the Assembly Hall (now the Paul Daisley Hall) would be wonderfully decorated with flowers and shrubs, fountains and ornamental designs that gladdened the heart on those cheerful occasions.

It was no surprise when, on the formation of the Borough of Brent in 1964, he was appointed to do the same job for the new, larger district – which he did with considerable distinction, as I will now recount.

First of all, he continued the Wembley practice of providing trees and shrubs for landscape work throughout the council's area, in its different office buildings and parks. He had to cover about 1,000 acres of parkland alone. He then extended the concept to the large range of housing developments, including high-rise, with street trees, flower beds and shrubs – the Chalkhill estate is one example out of many. He said 'these buildings may not be described as beautiful but they do provide some scope for open space around'.

He brightened grass verges (though too many of them now suffer from the effects of car parking churning up the otherwise welcome greenery), school playing fields and 'every other patch of council-owned land where a flower blooms or a tree flourishes' as the *Wembley Observer* reporter wrote in 1973.

Under his direction, the Brent Parks Department became one of the best run in London, though he had to deal with a severe shortage of skilled work people. By using new techniques he was able to operate with about half the number of staff which he employed when he started the job.

His inventive mind created an automatic irrigation system which was first used at Barham Park and was then installed at the Royal Gardens at Sandringham, at Kew Gardens, at the Royal Horticultural Society's gardens at Wisley – a notable success – and elsewhere. He went on to develop new land drainage techniques – a capillary-syphon system. This led to enquiries from Canada where sports enthusiasts hoped it would help speed up the drying out of pitches and thus lengthen the playing season. He extended the use of containers for trees and shrubs which reduced the need for manual labour and at the same time produced a higher quality of material.

We may think of vandalism as an unpleasant modern horror – with ASBOs and other crime prevention methods brought into play – but Leonard Chilcott was not discouraged forty years ago. Rather than make a fuss, he relentlessly replaced plants as fast as they were destroyed. 'Eventually people become used to having these things as part of their environment and the vandalism stops […] One thing to be learned from horticulture is patience – it is essential.' Brave words from a wise and dedicated servant of the people of Brent.

The quality of his professionalism made him a welcome speaker at horticultural conferences and gatherings. He was rewarded by his professional body, the Royal Horticultural Society with the Associateship of Honour which is conferred on British citizens who have rendered distinguished service in that field. In 1972, at the award ceremony, the president of the society quoted his many achievements and concluded, 'in all these ways you have enhanced both the art of horticulture and your own undoubted claims to our Associateship of Honour'.

The following year, well-satisfied with his work in Brent and the wonderful legacy around him, he retired – at first to his Sudbury home and then back to Somerset. The strange conclusion to this story is that no one I asked in and around Brent could remember when he died and it took a trip to the Family Records Centre and then a letter to the Registrar at Taunton to find out that he had died peacefully of natural causes on 4 February 1976 at Burnham-on-Sea, near where he was born. During that year, I was Mayor of Brent and the Parks Department won nineteen out of twenty categories in the annual 'London in Bloom' competition. What a tribute to his good work. Brent went on to build a marvellous horticultural nursery at Birchen Grove, named in his honour, although, some twenty years later, sadly it had to be sold off.

About the time he was ending his life in Somerset, a young man was starting out a life in horticulture at the Bridgewater Horticultural College – his name is Shaun Faulkner, now Leonard Chilcott's worthy successor as head of the Parks Department in Brent.

Trobridge – Architect Extraordinary

If you stand at the crossroads of Buck Lane and Wakeman's Hill Avenue in Kingsbury (near the highest point in Brent), you are immediately aware of something special. The buildings at the four corners are exciting to look at, unusual in design; they capture the imagination, they make you wonder about the person who designed them. They are each decorated, significantly, with a crusader's cross.

What is even more striking, is that, a short distance away along Buck Lane, is a string of thatched houses that look as if rural England had been planted in suburban London – as indeed the district was, in the 1920s. Yet, it was the same architect who was responsible. It is to the eternal credit of Brent Archives that, in 1982, they 'discovered' the genius of Ernest George Trobridge and put him firmly on the architectural roll of honour.

He was born on 23 April 1884 (320 years after William Shakespeare!) in Belfast. His father was head of the School of Design and was also a writer on and follower of the philosophy of Emmanuel Swedenborg (who also inspired William Blake), which enthusiasm he passed on to his son. Ernest went on to train as an architect, but Swedenborg's ideas clearly guided him throughout his life and inspired his work.

Highfort Court – one of Ernest Trowbridge's 'follies' in Buck Lane, Kingsbury, built in the 1930s.

In 1908 he came to London and soon had contracts to design buildings, though housing was soon to become his life's work. Through his philosophy, he was attracted to the idea of the co-partnership society – an early form of co-operative housing.

He married Jennie Pulsford (he carried out work for her father's building firm) in 1912 and they went to live in Golders Green in a house he had designed. With the outbreak of war, he found himself restricted in the work he could do and took up market gardening. The family moved to Haydon House in Kingsbury to escape the bombing in the First World War. This later became the centre from which he developed his ideas on housing design and the convenient location to supervise the projects which he undertook in the next twenty years.

As the war ended and the troops returned home, Trobridge realised there would be a housing problem. He was not alone in this, of course. Lloyd George, the Prime Minister, said 'the task was to make Britain a fit country for heroes to live in' and set up a committee to advise on building houses for the working classes – the Tudor Walters Committee, which set the standards for the next forty years (until Parker Morris). Trobridge invented and patented a number of key ideas which he saw as improvements on the traditional methods of house construction. Among these was a method of using green elm wood and for fire safety in thatched roofs.

At the *Daily Mail* Ideal Home Exhibition of 1920, he exhibited one of his timber-framed thatched-roofed houses and the government was shaken by the strength of his design and its comparative cheapness. Unfortunately, political decisions (national and local) delayed his progress and he was financially in difficulty for a time. However, he purchased ten acres at the junction of Kingsbury Road and Slough Lane and completed ten houses in 1922. They cost £775 each – about 20 per cent cheaper than conventional brick.

Then, during the 1920s and '30s, much of his work was in this area, but his commissions ranged across the country – Purley, Rye, Putney as well as nearby Colindale. There was one marvellous hotel in Canvey Island called Ozonia – sadly no longer in existence. In 1922 his wife

Ernest Trobridge and his family outside the house he built in Hay Lane, Kingsbury.

and their six children moved into Hayland (which he had originally built for his father) and then to Midcot, built next door. He was certainly one of the few architects who were willing to live in their own creations!

His work continued with the Summit estate in Buck Lane. His ideas were compared favourably with the contemporary French architectural genius Le Corbusier. Trobridge's houses were described as having 'the attributes of the new architecture with a friendly and familiar presence'. There is a variety in his house designs which is unlike that of any other comparable architect.

He continued building into the 1930s at Ash Tree Dell and other houses in Buck Lane. Then came what I regard as his masterpieces, though some styled them Trobridge's Follies. On the theme that the Englishman's home is his castle, he built fortified-style blocks of flats – the ones I referred to at the beginning of the article. Striking as they are to look at from the outside, they are comfortable inside (even though not without some minor problems, I am told). Here are Rochester Court and Highfort Court; Tudor Gates and Whitecastle Mansions. Look on them and marvel.

With the outbreak of war again in 1939, his work once more was halted. Three years later he died of diabetes at the early age of fifty-eight. His work then remained ignored by the professionals until, in the late 1970s, Geoff Hewlett of the Brent Planning Department helped designate Buck Lane and Slough Lane Conservation Areas, drawing attention to Trobridge's work. This led Val Bott, then curator of the Grange Museum and Archives and GP Smith of the Oxford Polytechnic Department of Architecture to set up an exhibition of his work. This is established Trobridge's reputation once and for all as an Architect Extraordinary.

A Bearing on the Matter

Among the shoppers at Sainsbury's in Glacier Way at Alperton, there will be some like the author's wife, who – just a few years earlier – would have been walking on that very site which was then the shop floor of a very large manufacturing company. The name of the road (suggested by the author) gives the game away. The firm was the Glacier Metal Company. So, how did it change from a large firm making bearings for engines to a firm like B&Q which used to sell bearings here for DIY users?

In 1899, two Americans who had settled in England, C.W. Findlay and A.J. Battle, formed a company called Findlay Motor Metals Ltd. After a visit to Switzerland in 1901, Findlay remarked at the likeness of molten white metal to a glacier. Thus, the new name 'Glacier Anti-Friction Metal Company' came into being. Today we would describe the product as plain bearings. By this time, Mr Battle had gone back to America, leaving the Findlay Company, now Glacier Metal Company, in control of the works. During the First World War they made die castings for hand grenades – a rather startling difference from the giant bearings fitted to an ocean-going liner, for which they later became famous in the engineering world. The war, with its development of the use of motor vehicles, gave an impetus for their return to the manufacture of bearings, in a factory in Waldo Road (just on the Hammersmith side of the Harrow Road at College Park).

In 1923, the firm moved to a muddy field alongside the Grand Union Canal at Alperton. It was not quite a vacant site. They took over the former works of the Wooler factory. That is romance in itself. The building (later known as 'The Cottage') had been used by John Wooler to make motorcycles, having moved there from his works in Wells House Road off Old Oak Common Road. His famous machine was the twin two-cylinder 'Flying Banana'. It had a distinctive yellow stripe on its petrol tank from which it got its nickname. About 2,000 of these lovely machines were produced before the factory closed in 1924, when the expanding Glacier firm took over its site.

Glacier House, Ealing Road, Alperton – the headquarters of the large bearing manufacturing firm until they moved out in the 1990s.

Wilfred Brown, who was born on 29 November 1908, joined them in 1931 when it was still a small firm, and in 1939 became chairman and managing director. He was responsible for initiating within the firm what became a renowned programme of research and development in organisation and management techniques, especially concerned with industrial relations reform. It was closely studied not only by managers and workers in the factories but also by academics like Professor Elliott Jacques who wrote a famous study in 1952, *The Changing Culture of a Factory*. Brown also published his own research in books like *Exploration in Management* in 1960 and together they founded the Glacier Institute of Management which made a substantial contribution to the philosophy of industrial organisation.

Brown was a confirmed socialist, and when Harold Wilson won the general election in 1964, he offered him the post of export minister, and made him a life peer. This meant he had give up his post at Glacier, though his influence long remained. He died in March 1985, survived by his wife Marjorie and his three sons.

Under Brown's leadership, the firm continued to develop new techniques and improved bearing products. They experimented with new materials like PTFE (polytetrafluoroethylene - simple if you break it down into its components!), bronze-lead, aluminium-tin and so on. The firm produced its DU bearing and a method of replacing bearings in large ships without having to put them into dry dock. The company expanded on both sides of the Ealing Road. They even constructed a pedestrian underpass beneath the main road to enable staff to move safely between the two parts of the site.

Many of the people who worked there lived locally – as did the author's wife for example. It came to them as a great shock when in the early 1990s the whole factory closed down and its work was transferred elsewhere – even though there had been rumours as early as 1972. What had been happening was typical of the enormous changes that have affected industries across the world – it was of course multinationalism. Glacier was taken over by Associated Engineering in 1964, though it was allowed to remain relatively unchanged. Later on, another large engineering

Lord Wilfred Brown, long-term chairman of Glacier Metal. (Courtesy of Brunel University)

conglomerate, Turner and Newall acquired it. Then – and this led to its departure from Alperton – it linked with an American multinational (a sort of reversion to its original links). Farewell Glacier from Alperton, though its name continues elsewhere.

There is a lovely twist to the story. Where Glacier Metal workers proudly worked their lathes and boring tools, until recently DIY-ers would shop at B & Q Store or harassed housewives (and husbands) trail round Sainsbury for their weekly shopping. However, up at the Town Hall, you can see the munificent municipal gift from the company, along with similar ones from Guinness and Heinz. These are the mayoral insignia. The famous craftsman Stuart Devlin designed the mayor's badge and chain for the Borough of Brent in 1965 in 18-carat gold and enamel and this was presented by the Arthur Guinness Company of Park Royal. Glacier presented the mayoress' badge and Heinz, whose factory was also at Park Royal at that time, presented the badges for the deputy mayor and mayoress.

My wife and I were at the presentation to the council of these regalia – a proud moment, which linked the civic and the industrial aspects of Brent in an indissoluble unity. Glacier (and Guinness and Heinz) will be long remembered, not only for their contribution to the commercial strength of Brent but also for their public generosity.

Stephenson and the First Mainline Railway

George Stephenson (1781-1848) is best known for the creation of the famous locomotive the Rocket and the Liverpool-Manchester Railway. He handed on his great skill to his son Robert (1803-1859) who began work in 1823, with his father as the first locomotive builder in the country. He went on to work in South America and returned to help his father in the railway business. Their lasting fame – and the local glory in our district – derives from building the London-Birmingham Railway.

In the latter part of the eighteenth century, the building of inland waterways – navigation canals – transformed the country and became an integral part of the Industrial Revolution. However, their most active life was barely fifty years before they were outclassed by a more formidable, and faster, form of mass transport – the railways. George Stephenson, the great Geordie who graces our five-pound banknotes, established himself as the brilliant railway engineer who brought about this change.

In the early part of the nineteenth century, he trained himself in the design of steam engines to transform them from operating stationary pumps to moving vehicles. He went on to create rail transport with the first public passenger train from Stockton to Darlington, hauled by his own engine. His next move was to build the Rocket which powered the trains from Manchester to Liverpool, in 1830.

The time was now ready for trunk railways. Robert Stephenson took up the challenge, advised by his illustrious father. With London as the focal point, an attempt was made to build a railway from London to Birmingham. Parliament insisted (as it still does) on sanctioning the railway and protecting the landowners from exploitation (though it turned out the boot was often on the other foot – the landowners often did very well out of the railway companies – Lord Northwick among them). In 1833 Stephenson and his backers succeeded at last in getting their Bill passed – though they had to pay up to the high price of £320 an acre. With himself as consultant and his son Robert as chief engineer to the London and Birmingham Railway, the new company went ahead laboriously acquiring the land. They had to get a 'yes' or 'no' from every owner and occupier on the route and then negotiate the price. John Copland and William Sellon, as well as Lord Northwick were among those giving the approval vote.

Willesden Junction Station, one of the major railway sites on the London & North Western Railway.

Stephenson's own engineering company submitted their estimate for the cost of construction – £2.5 million for seven years of work. The actual builders of the section from Camden (the original terminus) to the Brent River were Thomas Jackson and James Sneddon, while J.J. Ward and Jonathan Howell undertook the next sector to Bushey. The great seven-arched viaduct over the Brent valley (where the North Circular Road now runs, the river itself in a culvert) was one of the masterpieces of construction, standing the test of time, now over 170 years old. It is 30-50ft high, and more than 100,000 cartloads of earth were brought from the Oxhey cutting to make the embankments here. The workers – 'navvies', from the term navigation canals – included many Irish, who often came over to work on the harvest.

The contracts for the land often required the railway company to buy more than needed – a whole field, instead of half. The farmer, well compensated, then leased back the corner of his land now not needed by the railway. A local publication complained in 1837:

> Although it may be confessed, from a mercantile point of view, the railroads may prove of very great benefit yet … [we] regret that the fair face of England is to be seamed and scarred by the great giant commerce and the pure atmosphere of the country contaminated by the noxious vapours necessarily arising from the steam engines!

The first station out of Euston (land near the present terminus was taken up for the original starting point) was at Harrow and the first section to Boxmoor (near Hemel Hempstead) was opened on 6 July 1837 – a few months after Queen Victoria had come to the throne. A station at Willesden came in 1842 – it was actually near the present Harlesden Station and was used by the line's general manager, Capt Mark Huish, who lived in Harlesden House on Acton Lane, to get him to work at Euston every day. The station's porter-guard-ticket collector was known as Old Spinks and he lived in a nearby cottage, looking after the two platforms, level crossing and the three trains a day. Sudbury Station came in 1844 – but that was actually on Wembley High

Robert Stephenson, son of the first railway genius, who built the London to Birmingham Railway, later absorbed by the London & North Western. Courtesy of National Railway Museum)

Road, and the level crossing was removed shortly after, when the road was skewed to the north and a bridge erected, giving us the arrangement we have today – with the old coal yards long since removed with the decline of coal fires. And George Stephenson? He died in 1848 – as the five-pound note tells us – full of honours and with the booming railway industry the evidence of his success. Robert was elected Conservative MP for Whitby in 1847, but retired in 1859 due to ill health and died in the same year.

The King of Alperton

Some years ago we met some local people, proud of their roots and young Alan stayed with us for a week or so. We talked about his family and he took us to show a road, off the Ealing Road named in honour of the founder of the family – Haynes Road.

Henry Haynes was described in 1888 in an evening newspaper as 'a sort of Pooh Bah of trade, being in one person the landlord, publican, grocer, butcher, shoemaker and employer of labour for the district'. The article could have added half-a-dozen other jobs in which this jack-of-all-trades became involved.

He was born in 1831, right there in Alperton, the son of a local hay-dealer, James Haynes; as a boy he began work as a bellows-blower in the local blacksmith's – there was one in every village in those far-off days. Later he built a smithy of his own! He went on to build almost all of Alperton village in the latter part of the nineteenth century.

Alperton Station, on what was then called Alperton High Street (now Ealing Road), 1920. Most of the other buildings were part of the Haynes 'empire'.

He was so much in charge of the district that he issued his own coinage, which his employees then had to use as currency in his shops. It was actually a not uncommon practice at the time. The checks, or tallies, ranged in value from a penny to two shillings and consisted of zinc discs about the size of a modern ten-penny coin with the value and the name 'H HAYNES' impressed on them. Questions were asked in Parliament (as the phrase goes) and the home secretary of the day looked into it, but not much happened. It took until 1940 before the practice, was abolished, under the Truck Acts. I would liked to have told you that the home secretary in question was Henry Chaplin, after whom Chaplin Road in Wembley is indeed named, but that was a coincidence too far – he was agriculture minister at the time!

Henry Haynes went on to build a public house, an hotel (the Alperton Park Hotel to which he and his family moved in 1866 – it has undergone a number of name changes in recent years, but the original shape of the building can just about be discerned), cottages (some were in the road which now bears his name – others were Burns and Cromwell Roads), shops along Watery Lane (as the Ealing Road was significantly called in earlier days) and a chapel. He also worked a brickyard and sawmill which were very important to him in his role as builder of Alperton. At one time he owned seventy out of the one hundred buildings in the village. He employed almost the whole of the working population of Alperton – about 150 people. He supplied the village with water from his own well-house in Stanley Avenue

He had a business card in which he called himself 'a boat-builder' – his barges travelled between Alperton and Paddington Basin. He was into almost every local enterprise – which reads like a what's what of work: wheelwright, wharfinger, carpenter, builder, smith, farrier, manufacturer of stoves and ranges, and supplier of building materials, coal and coke. He built Alperton School – the first in the district – in 1876; it later became the Brent Teachers' Centre. It is now being redeveloped as a Hindu Temple.

C.J. Gueran, newsagent's shop at 402 Ealing Road, Alperton in 1911.

A group of Haynes' workmen, *c.* 1910.

Wembley Councillor E.J. Butler.

He and his wife, Harriet Martin – whose family came from Ireland – had seventeen children (some records say twenty-one).

Their eldest son, William, emigrated to Canada and their eldest daughter Isabel later in her life to New Zealand. The second surviving son, Harry, became one of the first Wembley District Councillors in 1894. He often found himself at loggerheads with his Kingsbury counterpart, T.S. Anderson – so much so that it led to the break up of the council into two separate units – Kingsbury and Wembley.

Henry Haynes was a big, dominant, self-made person, who never learned to read or write. He did manage to sign cheques – to pay his workers their wages. His daughter, Sarah Atkins, recalled that her father would hand the cheque to one of his workers who would then take a pony and trap to the bank in Paddington. The driver would put the money, for safe keeping, in the horse's nosebag, where the local policeman would find it, when, as often happened, the driver had taken a little too much to drink on the way home to Alperton.

He was a real patriarch – not only to his family but also to the village. He died in 1910 at the great age of seventy-nine. He and his wife are buried in St John's churchyard in Wembley. There is a permanent reminder in Haynes Road, off Ealing Road, which was proposed by Martin Curley, former Wembley Councillor and editor of Curley's *Wembley Directory*. Many descendants of Henry Haynes must be proud of their ancestor who created the beginnings of the modern Alperton.

two

Artistic Licence

'Wakey Wa-a-a-key!'

If you remember television in the 1960s, one show that is unforgettable was *The Billy Cotton Band Show*. The exuberant opening cry from the larger-than-life presenter of 'Wakey Wakey' would waken anyone slumbering before their screen as the band led into Billy's signature tune 'Somebody Stole My Gal'.

William E. Cotton spent much of his early married life in what is now Brent, but he was born at 1 Smith Square Westminster (coincidentally, opposite the former offices of the Conservative Party and where the Labour Party also had its headquarters for some years). His parents, Joe and Sukey, had ten children and Billy was the youngest, born on 6 May 1899. Joe was a turncock with the Metropolitan Water Board. Billy went to the local primary school (where he shone at football) and sang in the choir at St Margaret's – which is next door to Westminster Abbey.

With the outbreak of the First World War in 1914, he saw the chance to escape a humdrum life and – forgive the pun – tried to join up as a drummer and bugler, but was too young. A little later he made it and then found himself caught up as a fighting soldier in the Gallipoli campaign. On returning to England he found his family had moved to Kilburn. He did not stay long, as the desire to be active in the war was strong and he joined the Royal Flying Corps (soon to become the Royal Air Force). His love of flying stayed with him for the rest of his life – he did some of his flying at Stag Lane when the family had moved to Birchen Grove, Kingsbury, in the early 1930s. His younger son, Bill Cotton remembers (in his autobiography *Double Bill*) moving with his elder brother Ted, to the house in Birchen Grove. Later on they made their home at the large house at 262 Willesden Lane – which has since been redeveloped by the council as a block of flats named 'Pharamond'.

After the war, he became a bus conductor based at Cricklewood Garage and in 1921 married a Willesden girl, Mabel Gregory; they went to live in a flat in Kilburn Lane. He developed his love for speed by buying a motor bicycle with his RAF gratuity – and others followed. At about the same time he started in the music world, playing drums for different bands. Not content with that, he played football for Brentford and for Wimbledon and cricket for Wembley. He worked for a while at the motor car manufacturers, Bentley in Oxgate Lane, Neasden. He extended his other interests. He took up flying again and took lessons at de Havilland's at Stag Lane – where he met Amy Johnson (then training to be an aircraft engineer and pilot) and Will Hay the comedian and film star who shared with Billy a passion for flying. He bought a Gypsy Moth and used it to fly to dance engagements around the country.

His love of speed brought him contact with the enthusiasts of the fairly new motor-racing circuits and by 1935 he was into top-class motor racing, leading a marvellously active life – the favourite track at that time being Brooklands in Surrey. Bill won a wager by racing the famous Bluebird of Sir Malcolm Campbell. He wrote in his autobiography, *I Did It My Way*:

Billy Cotton and his London Savannah Band, 1925. (Courtesy of M.G. Thomas)

Billy Cotton enjoying his favourite pastime – motor racing at Brooklands in 1934.

It was only because I was a bandleader that I could afford to race motor cars. I tried to make my bookings coincide with my racing diary: If I was engaged for a Nottingham theatre, you could bet I had a race at Donington, and Liverpool would spell Southport Sands. But it would have to be a London engagement that allowed me to spend the Saturday at Brooklands.

At the start of his band career, he adopted the signature tune which was to be with him thereafter: 'Somebody Stole My Gal'. One of the first bands he worked with was that of his nephew Laurie Johnson who organised several bands to play during the British Empire Exhibition at Wembley in 1924 and 1925. He then started his own, the London Savannah Band, which was soon joined, in 1925, by his pianist and arranger, Clem Bernard who became a permanent fixture – and stayed for over forty years with the Cotton band.

Billy Cotton developed as a band leader and he was soon playing in the big London dance halls and night clubs, including the Astoria in Charing Cross Road and Ciro's. By the mid-1930s he had created his show band which was saucy, racy, raucous and hugely popular. His records included songs such as 'She Was Only Somebody's Daughter' and 'New Tiger Rag'. But in 1931 he became quite ill with rheumatic fever and the band (which included Nat Gonella, Sid Buckman and Syd Lipton) temporarily split up. He soon resumed, as strong as ever, playing, recording and, of course, motor racing.

During the Second World War he did a lot of work with ENSA (the services entertainment organisation) playing to service people in the Air Training Corps – his earlier links with the RAF tied in usefully. He was also responsible for the Sunday radio show, with the same name as the heading. *The Billy Cotton Band Show* became one of the most popular on television from 1957 to 1962, with the familiar blend of raucous good humour, good music and lively singing – his singers included the veteran Alan Breeze and Kathy Kay (who became very close to him for many years) and Rita Williams. It may seem tame by today's standards, but a great hit was 'I've got a Lovely Bunch of Coconuts!' He was Show Business Personality of the Year in 1962. He then suffered a stroke which slowed him down, but he carried on working. He collapsed watching a boxing match at the Wembley Arena in March 1969 and was taken to Wembley Hospital, where he was pronounced dead. After the funeral service at St Margaret's, where he had been a choirboy, he was cremated at Golders Green Crematorium. His great rousing call to start the show – 'Wakey Wa-a-key' would not be heard again.

George Morland – Painter of Rural Life

If I am not doing his memory a disservice, I want you to imagine Oliver Reed as a famous painter in the eighteenth century – a rumbustious, hell-raising, drinking companion with a certain genius at his craft. He could well have played George Morland, whose life would make a fascinating film script.

The first thing to remember is that at the time Morland was alive, at the end of the eighteenth century, Willesden was a country area, Marylebone was a village on the edge of London and the city itself was roughly the area within today's Inner Ring Road, north of the river (the Euston Road, then known as the New Road, had been built just a few years before he was born). In describing Morland as a painter of rural life, the objects of his attention were often quite near to his home ground.

He was born in Haymarket on 26 June 1763, where his father's house was one of a number in the midst of a growing entertainment area, which it still is today. His father Henry Morland was a painter of some distinction in his time and his French-born mother was also quite a competent artist. It does not surprise us to learn that George's boyhood was not a happy one. His father, despite, or perhaps due to, his artistic temperament was an austere, dominating tyrant. His two brothers ran away to sea to escape the unhappy home. Freud, one hundred years later, would have totally understood the boy's distressful upbringing. He was shy and turned to music and painting to compensate for his unhappy environment. His skill with the paintbrush became his better skill (though his fiddle playing remained with him throughout his life and he often enlivened his inn carousals with his style of music playing).

Through his father, he met some of the great painters of the day – the young John Flaxman and the older Thomas Gainsborough (who helped found the Royal Academy) and Joshua Reynolds among them. He learned from and was inspired by them and soon became one of the foremost artists of the English artistic world - recognised by them and by others like George Romney, the portrait painter of Emma Hamilton. He left home and set up house in Bow Street, but was soon to be found, too often, in taverns like the Cheshire Cheese off Fleet Street.

He was an attractive, jovial and sporting-looking fellow, as he was described, of good humour and with a daring and adventurous spirit. These traits got him into many scrapes and drunken brawls. He was always short of money, although his painting skills would frequently come to his rescue as he could turn out a good picture very rapidly and make a little money that way.

He met and went to live with a skilful engraver, William Ward, who lived at Kensal Green – then a hamlet way outside the busy life of London town. Paintings were often engraved and thus became better known throughout fashionable society even if the originals were barely known. William and George both had sisters and a double wedding took place, William to Maria Morland and George to Anne Ward. They set up house together but it did not last long and George and Anne moved to Camden Town. He continued to paint scenes of country life; of children and of work people. He was a radical and today would have been seen as a bohemian left-winger who despised (even though he painted for) the wealthy.

Anecdotes about him are legendary. He was asked to paint an inn sign for the landlady of the Coach and Horses in Stonebridge (the inn – not the original building of course – which has now been demolished and redeveloped as flats). Then he went and lost it and could not go back there to claim his fee. On another occasion, (as F.W. Blagdon tells us in a biography published soon after Morland's death) Lord Derby came to call when the artist was living in the Edgware Road in order to buy a picture from him. Morland called out from the garret window 'oh, d—n Lords, I paint for no Lords: shut the door, Bob ...' (to one of the associates of his gang who 'guarded' him from intruders). His faithful wife was sorely tried by his antics. Roger Quilter wrote an opera about his love life entitled *Love at the Inn*.

Morland seems to have been the first painter to prefer not to paint to the orders of customers but he chose to produce works in his own studio, at his own expense and sell them through an

George Morland – self-portrait from around 1795. (Courtesy National Portrait Gallery)

The William IV Inn, Harrow Road, reputedly one of Morland's haunts and the subject of some of his paintings – probably called the George III in his time in recognition of the ruling monarch.

agent or gallery. Among his thousands of paintings is one which is believed to be of the Plough Inn which used to be on the Harrow Road at Ladbroke Grove. 'Le Halte', which is in the Louvre in Paris, bears the sign of The Bell on Kilburn High Road. Morland also painted the other famous inn on our stretch of the Edgware Road – in the Tate Gallery there is the painting, 'At the Door of the Red Lion'.

He was always too generous when he had money and was often fleeced by greedy art dealers, so that he was frequently in debt. There is no doubt that much of his work was that of an artist painting in a hurry in order to met the demands of his creditors but there are many pictures which should be brought out from the store rooms of the great art galleries like the Tate and shown to the public for us to gauge his real worth. He died of a brain fever, unsurprisingly, in a detention house for debtors on 29 October 1804 aged forty-two. His earlier fame by now counted for little. Only after his death was his fame restored.

Brent's Mr Music

I bet that many of you – and not just the older readers like me – know the foot-tapping, lyrical song, 'Lady of Spain': 'Lady of Spain, I adore you/Right from the night I first saw you'. It was the greatest hit of a highly successful twentieth-century songwriter who lived most of his life in Willesden and thus justly earned his title, from one of the local newspapers of the time, 'Brent's Mr Music'.

Tolchard Evans, though from a Welsh family, was born in Paddington in 1901 and was one of a large family of boys and girls, though he was brought up by his grandmother. I am indebted to one of his sisters, the late Marguerite Evans (herself a well-known local painter) for information about him and the loan of a family album – an act of rare generosity. I also acknowledge the contribution of Mark White in his book on popular songwriters, *You Must Remember This* (Frederick Warne, 1983).

Tolchard moved to Willesden as a young boy and, I believe, went to Chamberlayne Road School. Later, after he married, he moved with his wife Phyllis to Hardinge Road, between Chamberlayne Road and All Souls Avenue. They lived there for about forty-six years until his death in March 1978.

During the First World War, in 1916, he started working as an office boy – where else but in Tin Pan Alley (Denmark Street, off Charing Cross Road) which in those days was the centre for many of the music publishers of the day. He was fortunate enough to start work with the famous Lawrence Wright, who used a pen name for his own highly successful song-writing career – the name Horatio Nicholls ('Among My Souvenirs', 'When the Guards are on Parade' and 'Amy, Wonderful Amy' – about the famous aviator, Amy Johnson). It was not long before the young

Tolchard embarked on his own intended career in music; one of the first of his to be published is the long-forgotten 'Candlelight'.

He began another, parallel, career as a pianist-band-leader in 1925, in Westcliff-on-Sea, then moving to the Queen's Hotel in Southend. There, in 1926, he wrote his first best-seller 'Barcelona' ('I'm one of the Knuts of Barcelona...'). Evans recounted to a local journalist in Southend that he went on to the pier to see if he could create something like 'Valencia' (another earlier hit by a different writer) 'and, while riding on the tramway [Southend Pier was three miles long] the rhythm and the tune suddenly came to me. It was born by the gentle swaying and blessed by the breezes over the Estuary'. His greatest hit was, probably, 'Lady of Spain' written in 1931, while another, 'If', was popularised by the American star Perry Como. Yet another of his successes which many will remember from seaside concert parties and at sing-alongs, was 'Let's All Sing Like the Birdies Do – Tweet, Tweet, Tweet' which, amazing to recall now, also sold over a million copies.

Following his success at Southend, he found himself with a wider audience in BBC radio, in the 1940s and 1950s – for example a series called *The Tuneful Twenties*. Tolchard was also able to use his connections with other songwriters, dating from his time in Tin Pan Alley, to good effect in programmes such as this. He said about another programme, *The Friendly Invasion* (about American song-writing) that 'it wasn't at all friendly – I had to fight all the way for my living. I realised it would be useless to write songs in the same style as Irving Berlin or George Gershwin – but it was tough fighting off the mighty dollar and the American films'. His idol was Jerome Kern. He was later to win several Ivor Novello awards for his song-writing – a just tribute from his fellow British artists.

As a young man of eighteen, he played the piano in a club in Chamberlayne Road (around the corner from the house he was later to own). This was the Kensal Rise Conservative Club. A headline in the local paper in January 1978 revealed the truth: 'Tolchard, the tuneful Tory, gets life membership' – although, after all that time since he first played there, 'life' was only a few months more, as he died in March that year.

I would like to think that it that it was not a coincidence that the person who presented him with the special Ivor Novello Award in 1974 was the then Conservative MP (now Lord) Norman St John Stevas. It celebrated fifty years of service to the British music industry.

His obituary in the *Wembley Observer* in March 1978 recalled that he had written over 1,000 songs. By the time he died he was the oldest remaining British composer from Tin Pan Alley.

He is buried in Willesden New Cemetery. The interment was attended by his wife and two sons, other family and friends who included the songwriter Jimmy Kennedy ('Red Sails in the Sunset') with whom, by coincidence the author worked for a short while on a troopship during the war on the way to India, putting on a show. To write catchy tunes – the kind everyone can whistle – is a rare and exciting gift and Tolchard had that gift in abundance. Even if he is himself now largely forgotten, his best songs, like those of all the great tunesmiths, will always be here to remind us that the melody lingers on.

Zangwill – The Jewish Dickens

At 24 Oxford Gardens in the 1890s – which was at that time in Willesden (now, after boundary changes, in Westminster) – lived the Zangwill family. The head was Moses, a sixty-year old retired merchant who had been born in Latvia in what was then Russia, before emigrating to this country. His wife Ellen who had come from Poland was also on the 1891 census with their six children, born in this country – one of whom a twenty-seven-year old journalist was to become one of the best-known writers of his generation and one of the most remarkable of all British Jews.

Far left: Tolchard Evans. (Courtesy of the late Marguerite Evans)

Left: Israel Zangwill. (Courtesy of the Jewish Museum)

Israel Zangwill was brought up in a loving family but in great poverty. I called his father 'a merchant' – he was an old-clothes peddler who travelled round the country barely making a living. Israel was born in the East End – so delighted in referring to himself as a 'Jewish Cockney' – and went to the Jews' Free School then in Bell Lane Spitalfields. (It is now on a new site in Kingsbury). He became a teacher there and also started writing the first of his many books and stories.

During the 1880s there was a group of aspiring professionals who began to meet, quite informally in different houses in Kilburn and nearby. They called themselves 'The Wanderers of Kilburn' – because they wandered into each other's houses, they wandered from topic to topic and, of course they were Wandering Jews. They included the young Zangwill, the editor of *the Jewish Chronicle*, Asher Myers, lawyers, artists, scholars. They helped to create a lively atmosphere for Jewish cultural life at the end of the nineteenth century.

While living in the family house, Zangwill helped set up a group called the Maccabeans, which met in Piccadilly, and it was there that Zangwill met Theodor Herzl, the founder of modern Zionism. This was at a time of great mass migration, particularly of Jews fleeing the pogroms in Russia and then facing the inevitable backlash of anti-Semitism in England which culminated in the Aliens Act of 1905. Zangwill later moved into the argument for settling Jews who were escaping from oppression in any suitable territory in the world – which brought him later in contact with my grandfather, who had similarly broad views. He was involved in setting up the Jewish Territorial Organisation which looked for land other than in Palestine. Nonetheless, there is a plaque set up in 1965 on the wall of his old house in Oxford Road: 'In this house, Theodor Herzl came to see Israel Zangwill and modern Zionism was born, 21 November 1895'.

At the same time, Zangwill was busy writing stories, articles, plays and novels including his masterpieces *Children of the Ghetto* and *The King of the Schnorrers* (beggars). His plays were successful at the time, though less well-known now. His many friends included H.G. Wells, Bernard Shaw, Rudyard Kipling and many other writers and well-known people of the day. He was a supporter of women's suffrage and this brought him in touch with the woman who became his wife – Edith Ayrton. When he died in 1926, his obituary by Joseph Leftwich included this marvellous praise: 'as a great writer and as a great Jew, Zangwill seems to me an immortal'.

A Great Read

Popping down to the local library was not always as easy as it is today. Though there have been libraries of a kind since ancient times (one at Alexandria was famous before it was destroyed), the provision of free public libraries for everybody to use did not start until an Act of Parliament in 1850. Willesden then was a series of tiny villages and it took several attempts, towards the end of that century to get the idea going.

A democratic referendum in 1891 was organised by Councillor W.B. Luke and Mr W. North. By a two to one majority, the residents of Willesden agreed to spend a penny rate (all the law allowed – it provided £1,100) to build a library with two branches, in different parts of their parish. This was a little different from many other places where they voted for one main public library, but this was still a spread-out town with at least two other centres and one location would not have been acceptable.

Would you believe the words of one backwoodsman who wrote opposing the proposal: 'if public libraries are needed why cannot they be supported by those who need them backed by those philanthropists who wish to provide them'.

A Library Commission was set up to acquire sites and these were found at Willesden Green, Kilburn and Harlesden. Staff were recruited and one of these was a young man of twenty-one, Frank E. Chennell who applied for the post at each of the three branches and landed the one of Librarian at Willesden Green. He stayed there until 1937, having reached the post of Borough Librarian and one of the most respected in his profession in England.

It so happened that the first to open was the one at Kilburn. It had been designed by the architects Edmeston and Gabriel and held 4,000 books. For the opening ceremony, the Library Commission succeeded in inviting as the distinguished guest, the head of Harrow School, Revd James E.C. Welldon (who went on to become Bishop of India and then Dean of Manchester and of Durham). Two weeks later, on 14 February 1894, Harlesden (designed by a local architect Mr John Cash) declared itself open to the public. The ceremony, which revealed a stock of 6,000 books, was performed by a distinguished scientist, Sir Henry Roscoe, Professor of Chemistry at Manchester University. He had worked with von Bunsen (the inventor of the Bunsen burner, still used in every school laboratory today) and had been MP for South Manchester.

At the last but of course not the least was the Willesden Green Library designed by the brothers Newman and Newman (who had designed the Willesden Cottage Hospital among others) at a cost of £2,600 and with 5,000 books. This time the opening was carried out by the local MP, Mr I.E.B. Cox, whose constituency was – believe or not – Harrow, which stretched right down from Pinner to Kilburn!

Imagine going to choose a book. There was no 'open access', you could not just wander round, look at the books, deciding which to take out. You had to look at a catalogue and then the librarian would refer to an indicator to see if the book was still available or out on loan! A specimen of this old-fashioned device is held at the Brent Local History Museum.

The success of these free libraries was such that agitation started soon after for a further branch at Kensal Rise. Land for this was generously given by All Souls College Oxford (who had owned much of the land in this part of the parish, as instanced by the road which bears its name, All Souls Avenue). The difficulty was that, with only a penny rate to play with, there was not enough money. This was the cry that would haunt the library service thereafter, and still does. The commission decided that only a reading room could be built to start with. When this had been made ready, they found that the famous American humorist, Mark Twain, was staying at Dollis Hill House, on one of his many visits to Europe and they persuaded him to open the room. This delightful occasion was repeated at the centenary celebration in September 2000, a look-a-like actor playing the part of the writer.

The happy start had a happier continuation. The famous benefactor, Dr Andrew Carnegie, was approached and he agreed to provide money to allow an extension so as to enable a fully sized local library to be built. This was carried out to the design of Mr A.H. Murray-Rust who

Kilburn Library, Salusbury Road – the first of three Willesden Libraries to open, in quick succession, pictured in 1894.

Brent Town Hall Library, c. 1975.

worked for the local firm of Done, Hunter of Cricklewood and, when complete, was opened by Judge Rentoul, KC, in May 1904.

Later, as the population expanded into the north of Willesden, branches opened in Cricklewood (which now houses the Local Archives) and Neasden. Curiously an area the size of Stonebridge has never been provided with its own public library, although the mobile library service has served the area well as it has done in Alperton.

Wembley never operated its own library service; until the formation of the Borough of Brent, it was part of the Middlesex County Library Service – which certainly provided a good and efficient network, with powers delegated to a local committee to oversee the function. The main library was created within the Town Hall and others were built at Ealing Road, Preston Road, Tokyngton, in the old Crab's House in Barham Park (see p.75) and in Kingsbury.

The libraries, over the years provided much more than the lending of books; free newspapers was one feature; work with children partly by activities within each library and also by linking up with schools. More recently there has been the lending of records, and then CDs, tapes and each successive new recording device. The libraries have become information centres not only for the supplying of factual details of local and other services but with the installation of computers, they link the individual reader (or 'customer') with the outside world of information. Libraries provide exhibition displays, organise reading groups, play-reading and record recitals. Willesden Green Library Centre, the rebuilt and greatly enlarged original Council Library has a coffee shop, cinema and now the Brent Local History Museum.

Today's library network, so well created by the previous local authorities, has, in recent years, often been under threat of closure, but public opinion, in support of its public libraries, has kept the network intact – in Brent, and I suspect in many other boroughs.

A Cosy Night at the Flicks

An evening out at the cinema is not the regular choice for many people today, but in the thirties of the last century, during the war and for about ten years after that, many families would pay a twice-weekly visit to the 'flicks'. Children were hooked on the habit by going to a Saturday morning matinee. For sixpence or a shilling each (three pence for children!), they would be taken away from the normality (and, in wartime, from the stresses and horrors of life) into a dream world of fantasy, fun and fiction.

The image of the picture palace (and this was often the right word to use) was carefully cultivated by the cinema owners – they wanted people to feel they were entering a haven for the world-weary and savouring the dark caverns of illuminated bliss.

The first organised film shows in Brent, seem to have been given in Willesden in April 1902 at the Constitutional Hall in St Mary's Road. Shown to large 'houses', for five nights a week, were cinematograph pictures of the cruise of the Prince and Princess of Wales, of the Japanese Navy and of the Royal Navy. These were described in the local paper as 'a fine exhibition of the latest scientific development of photography'.

The first regular cinema showings, used the Constitutional Hall, but it was advertised as animated pictures, twice nightly at 6.50p.m. and 9p.m. It was soon called 'The Premier Electric Theatre'. It was run by David Jamilly and Percy Gallagher and they claimed it was 'an entertainment that holds everybody. Plenty to laugh at. Nothing to shock you. Two hours' solid entertainment.' Front rows cost 1s and the back, 3d. Jamilly had to convince the customers that the cinema was respectable and so used to stand outside, dressed in a frock coat.

Savoy (Essoldo) Cinema, Burnt Oak. (Courtesy Cinema Theatre Association)

Other early cinemas in the district were in a building next to the Coach and Horses Inn – now the Caterers' Mart and in Cricklewood the Little Palace, opened in 1909. The People's Picture Palace was at 103 High Street Harlesden and there was another across the road at 120 High Street which later became the Picardy. They then followed thick and fast in the years before the First World War. 1912 – Omnium Electric Palaces Ltd (what delicious names they had in those days) opened the Rutland Park Cinema at 67 High Road Willesden Green as a super cinema to show the budding film world's exciting one-reelers. It had 500 seats – 1s for a reserved seat, with lounges and a tea garden. Wembley's first cinema was the Blue Hall at the junction of the High Road and Cecil Avenue – which I believe had originally been a skating rink.

Then there was the Coliseum at Harlesden (long since closed for films, but the name still preserved in a new guise); the Pavilion at Kensal Rise and nearby the Picture Palace. The Grange in Kilburn High Road opened in 1914 and twenty years later I saw my very first film there. Not to overlook the Savoy at Chapel End (another case of a cinema use long since fizzled out, but the building still in use for other purposes) and the Electric Theatre in Lonsdale Road in Kilburn.

When the cinema came to its peak years, the big circuits started to build their latest proud projects. Perhaps the best was the Odeon with its stylish modern lines – at Sudbury, Kenton, Kingsbury, Harlesden and Burnt Oak. The Regal in the Ealing Road was almost the last to go when the great decline set in. There was a Granada, part of the Bernstein empire (and Sidney Bernstein also came to own the Willesden Hippodrome (see p.49), sadly demolished by a bomb in the Second World War and never rebuilt). The Majestic in Wembley High Road was opened in 1929 on the site of the Copland Hospital in Wembley High Road; it had 1,500 seats, an organ, stage and room for a full orchestra. It was sold to the Odeon chain in 1960 and it was then pulled down to make way for a C & A shop in 1962 – when they, in turn, left it remained as a general store.

Visiting the cinema these days is more of an occasional treat than the regular weekly or even twice-weekly parade in years past. It now often involves a journey to find the nearest place showing a film of your choice. In the heyday of film-going, say fifty years ago, there would have been a cinema near you, often holding an audience of a thousand or more, with a programme that would include a 'big' picture, a second feature, a newsreel and some cartoons – a full programme. At some of the largest theatres there would be a stage show with comedians, singers a band and other acts. Four hours of entertainment were offered each time, some times twice a day and children's shows on Saturday mornings.

At the height of cinema fashion, there were some thirty cinemas in Brent – now there are only two, both fairly recently opened, in Willesden. The best of these was, undoubtedly, the Gaumont State which was planned in the 1930s to meet the insatiable demand, deliberately, located not in the West End but in a London suburb accessible to the centre.

George Cole, FRIBA, the famous cinema architect produced a number of designs one of which was accepted and which became the magnificent structure which we now know as the State. The site was at 197-199 Kilburn High Road – a comparatively narrow frontage but extending over a former works site behind and also along Willesden Lane. It was to have a landmark tower, 130ft high – quite sizeable at that time – to be illuminated at night.

An architect needs a developer to enable the scheme, however good, to be built. This was where the Hyams brothers, who had many contacts in the film world, came in. They were Philip, Sidney and Michael, usually known to their staff as Mr Phil, Mr Sid and Mr Mike – Philip died in 1998 at the grand age of 102. They undertook to see it built and while it is true that they ran out of money, they found help in a subsidiary of the large Gaumont British Picture Corporation whose subsidy saw the project through. That is how 'Gaumont' came to be part of the name of the cinema.

Metro (Willesden Green) Electric Palace, 1909.

Willesden County Court in 1961. In the 1880s it was Willesden Grammar School; in the 1920s it was a film studio.

At the beginning of the construction, a signboard was put up which proudly claimed 'The Largest Cinema in the World'. However, rather awkwardly, it turned out that they were building an even larger one – the Pantages Theatre in Los Angeles. They smartly amended the sign to read 'The Largest Cinema in Europe' and, at 4,004 seats, it thus maintained its dignity and accuracy.

The amazing architecture is Italianate in style, true Art Deco of the period and has rightly been granted a Grade Two Star status as a listed building. The attractive light-coloured frontage, with the tower stands out – you can see it, from a good vantage point, from miles around. However, it is the wonderfully elaborate foyer which distinguishes it from every other London cinema. The grand marble staircase is showered with light from the chandeliers – replicas of those at Buckingham Palace. As you enter it, it glitters with reflected light, shining from every marble surface – the whole foyer is an exquisite example of the fantasy world which Cole aimed to create. The myriad lights in the foyer and elsewhere in the large auditorium were looked after by a young electrician called Cecil ('Jim') Pike, who the author and his wife came to know when he retired to live in Wembley.

It was into this luxurious setting that the patrons, the cinema-goers walked in wonder to attend the first night on Monday 20 December 1937 (I missed the opportunity but went about a week later and was a regular visitor until war came in 1939). What a parade of 1930s talent was brought together for this special occasion – it was up to Hollywood standards. The crush of onlookers in the Kilburn High Road brought joy to Kilburn despite traffic congestion of almost Hollywood first-night proportions. The Guests of Honour, as they were called on the programme, included Gracie Fields, George Formby, Larry Adler, Vic Oliver, Carroll Levis, Vivian Van Dam and his State Orchestra and Sidney Torch at the great Wurlitzer organ. Wow! What a night of stars.

For about twenty-five years, the State lived up to its great reputation. The double feature film programme, stage show and the organ (with Sidney Torch, of course) resumed their popularity immediately after the war. Yet, with all the wonder of the building, the excitement you felt as you walked through the doors whether to the 9d-seats in the front or 1s 6d ones in the circle, even this magnificent cinema could not buck the trend of declining attendances which the advent of television had induced. They tried with a second screen built into the circle; they converted part of the hall to Bingo. Part of the cinema (it was so vast) was turned into a ballroom and Victor Sylvester and his band (see p.46) were among the musicians. It was in vain. The darkened auditorium stands as a sad memorial to the hopes and expectations of screen-worshippers, as a monument to the great days of show business, to the palace of dreams.

Just occasionally, a tour is arranged for the public (new and old) to see and walk up and down the grand staircase (which has featured in a number of films). In 1963 both the Beatles and the Rolling Stones played at the State Ballroom. There are occasional organ recitals and if you see any of these advertised go along and, echoing Bob Hope, say 'thanks for the memory'.

As we now know, it was all going to turn to tears and sorrow – at least in the film industry, though only for a while. Television, that new young upstart medium, almost killed off the cinemas. It succeeded in Brent, that is true and for a period of about twenty years there was not one cinema in the district. That we now have two is a minor miracle – the one inside the Willesden Green Library Centre (converted from an open-plan theatre) and the even more delightful Tricycle Cinema, built on the success of the only professional theatre in Brent.

There is just one more thing to add – a cliff-hanger, as in all the best cinemas. Did you know that Wembley nearly became the Hollywood of England?

Kingsbury Manor, 1969 – where Baird carried out his early experiments in television.

Baird's Exciting Experiment

The romantic story starts a hundred years ago in a corner of farmland near the village of Kingsbury. It was reached from London along the Edgware Road to the Hyde, then turning off into Kingsbury Lane, on past the Plough Inn to a spot not far from the legendary site of the Gore Moot). This was where the Duchess of Sutherland had her home.

Mary Caroline was the daughter of Dr Richard Michell (1805-1877), principal of Hertford College, Oxford - the college with the 'Bridge of Sighs'. She first married Arthur Kinnersley Blair and they had a daughter, Irene Mary who became Countess Bubna. After Arthur Blair's death, she became the second wife of George Granville Leveson-Gower, the 3rd Duke of Sutherland (1828-1892). After his death, she became, again, a second wife, this time to Sir Arthur Rollitt (who died in 1922) one time Lord Mayor of Hull and later MP for Islington from 1886 to 1906.

The Rollitts built themselves a Victorian country house in the land between Gore and Valley Farms in Kingsbury – a hideaway from the fraught life of Parliament twelve miles away in London. It was designed by the eminent architect W. West Neve and was known as the Cottage Manor House – George Cloke renamed it Kingsbury Manor in 1929 – and there it stands, on the edge of what is now Roe Green Park, its walled garden a council depot.

The Duchess (she was also known as Lady Blair) died in 1912, by which time her daughter, Countess Bubna, was using the cottage. When her stepfather, Arthur Rollins died in 1922, she had to give it up. In 1929, it was bought by the building contractor, George Cloke, who renamed it. He gifted it to the Middlesex County Council some ten years later. With the break up of the county in 1965, it came to Brent who used the Manor for offices, while the coach house, nearby, was given over to the Kingsbury Veterans' Club.

John Logie Baird. (Courtesy National Portrait Gallery)

I now go back to 1928. John Logie Baird, born in Helensburgh in 1888, was smitten with the concept of what Constantin Persky had named in 1900, 'Television'. He was one of a number of people world-wide working on the concept, many inspired by the early work of Paul Nipkow in Germany. Others included Philo T. Farnsworth (who appears in a novel about the American magician, *Carter Beats the Devil*) and Vladimir Zworkin who also worked in the USA. By the late 1920s, Baird had carried out a lot of work, but when the BBC declined co-operation, he set up his own transmitting station in the coach house of Kingsbury Manor. Masts were erected, although an air of secrecy had to be maintained and most of the important experiments were carried out at dead of night after sound broadcasting had ceased.

Baird was the first to achieve any form of television, over any distance, *The New York Times* graciously conceded in 1928. Prototype models of television receivers were made and tested at Kingsbury. Baird's chief engineer there, H.J. Barton-Chapple, recalled the big night in July 1929:

My assistant and I and our staff were grouped round the receiver lens. My heart pounded as we waited for our colleagues in Berlin to make contact. Heaven knows how Baird felt waiting at headquarters. Then came the familiar whirring sound through the ether. Our men in Berlin were coming through. And, upon my soul, so was an image on the screen. It was blurred at first, then it became a crude face – the face of a gnome with a pointed beard and a peaked hat; the kind of model you see in gardens. We had made it at last! I remember cheering and hugging my assistant with joy.

The system Baird had invented was based on a mechanical method, called the Televisor – and it worked. Some 20,000 sets were sold; by this time the BBC were, grudgingly, involved and it was possible to give up the use of the coach house at Kingsbury.

Baird was, however, not an easy convert to electronic television, preferring his mechanical system and he, in due course, had to concede that the BBC's preference for Farnsworth's system as improved by RCA and EMI's 600-line pictures was the future.

In 1953, the Queen was crowned; Everest was conquered and, on a bright July day, a large party of local Wembley people, the Assistant Postmaster General (a government junior minister responsible for the Post Office and Royal Mail in those days) and friends of Baird, gathered to pay the inventor tribute. A stone tablet (made by C.J. Corden, a local craftsman) was erected outside what is now the veterans' club, by the fledgling Wembley History Society under its enthusiastic chairman, Cllr Martin Curley. It says, as you can see for yourself:

> This stone commemorates the site of the masts used for the reception of the first television signals from the Continent by John Logie Baird, pioneer of television, in July 1929.

As we sit in front of our TV sets today, we are probably aware that the picture we see is produced electronically – the result of the choice of Zworkin's method rather than Baird's. But, Baird did not fail – he paved the way for the great revolution in sight and sound of the twentieth century – and he did the key work here in Kingsbury.

'Slow, Slow, Quick, Quick, Slow' – Began in Wembley

The young, just-married Revd John Silvester came to the village of Wembley in 1896 to be curate of the fifty-year old parish church of St John the Evangelist. It had been founded, with the aid of the Copland Sisters, in 1846, creating the parish of Wembley from the larger old district of Harrow.

Less than a year after his arrival, the then incumbent resigned and Revd John William Potts Silvester became vicar of Wembley. He was to hold that post until 1944 – longer than anyone before or since. He and his wife Kate brought up their large family in the vicarage, next to the church, described by his son, Victor, as 'a large, rambling, red-brick house standing back from a fine front garden, with an orchard at the back. Beyond that were open fields; Wembley in my childhood was just a small village'. The building has now gone and a new vicarage and a small estate of houses have taken the place of the orchard.

The young family consisted of: Temple, the eldest (named after Archbishop Frederick Temple), Gwen, Joyce, Mary and Joan and, in between, born on 25 February 1900 – the day on which good news of a victory in the Boer War was announced – was Victor Marlborough. The future dance band leader grew up in a Wembley which, as he described in the quotation above, had hardly begun to grow, despite the existence of a railway station connected to central London and the church – two essential elements in the creation of a stable community.

As Victor further recalls in his autobiography, *Dancing is my Life*, his father was 'a tall, good, kind-hearted man with a big moustache, but in religious matters a stern Victorian. He was sincere and well-intentioned … brought up his children rather strictly'. His mother was 'a tall and stately woman with a beautiful oval face and a fine figure. She was gentle and very devout … subscribed to the theory that children should be seen and not heard'.

They lived 'in a state of genteel poverty', but they had a cook, a housemaid and a governess. Victor recalls the sexton at the church, William Dell, 'a huge good-natured lumbering man', who would have been in his forties as young Victor was in his early years. Dell lived in the schoolmaster's cottage behind the church, which had been built by the Copland sisters.

Shortly before Revd Silvester came to Wembley, it so happened that the new Urban District Council was created. Although it is not common practice for ministers of the cloth to become involved in local government, it is not surprising that John Silvester, with his great sense of public duty, decided to become a councillor. He served from 1911 to 1926 and was chairman (no mayors for district councils) in 1921-22, to the great delight of his children. The road named for him is, curiously, misspelt as Sylvester Road.

Victor recalls, perhaps with some wry pride, some schoolboy pranks, often with the aid of his elder brother, Temple. On a Sunday, they climbed one of the horse chestnut trees – still there – whose overhung branches allowed them, concealed, to drop conkers on the heads of prominent members of the congregation, arriving in their top hats (presumably they did not dare assail the lady members).

Victor Silvester.

Victor Silvester. (Courtesy BBC)

On another occasion, at a children's party at Sudbury Lodge (later Barham Park Mansion) he was sitting next to another Victor, the ten-year old Victor Goddard, son of Dr Charles Goddard, the local GP and also Medical Officer of Health for the new District Council who lived in Harrowdene House opposite the vicarage. As the other Victor tilted back in his chair, glass of milk in hand, our Victor 'couldn't resist giving him a push which tipped him over backwards, spilling the milk all over his sailor suit'. Our Victor went on to become one of the most famous dance band leaders in the country – the other Victor became an Air Vice Marshall with a distinguished career in the RAF!

The biggest 'prank' of all was at the outbreak of the First World War when he ran away from his hated boarding school, Ardingly College, to join the army, aged fourteen years and nine months. He had managed to convince the recruiting officer that he actually old enough to join up. Within a few months, still only fifteen, he was fighting on the Western Front and took part later in the Battle of Arras. In 1917, he recalled, he was a member of a firing squad which shot four British soldiers sentenced to death for desertion and cowardice. Eventually wounded, he was discovered, still too young and brought home to Blighty.

This was the local lad who found in ballroom dancing his niche in life – world champion, band leader, and founder, in the Second World War of the morale-boosting 'BBC Dance Club'. After the war, the band did a lot of touring. The author's wife, Joan, worked for a time at the Majestic Ballroom in Wembley High Road and remembers him and his band playing there in the 1950s. With his Brylcreemed hair, his immaculate dress suit and ever-present smile he single-handedly created the vogue for ballroom dancing – which is now an Olympic sport!

Former Wembley Vicarage, boyhood home of Victor Silvester.

His famous slogan, quoted in the title, is still synonymous with ballroom dancing and the name of Victor Silvester lives on long after his death in 1978.

Hurrah for the 'Hipp' – Willesden's First Theatre

By the end of the nineteenth century, almost every town in England had a theatre. This was true of some of London's suburbs, where they provided good entertainment in comfortable surroundings at lower prices than in the West End – and it was local. The Victorians had a great thirst for drama, variety, opera and music-hall. The heyday of theatre building was the last quarter of that century, but, alas, most of the buildings have disappeared; with most being redeveloped and converted to bingo halls while a few remained as cinemas until they, too, were lost to the world of entertainment.

In Willesden, a bustling, rapidly expanding town from the 1890s, there were several proposals put forward by local business people who saw the advantages of such an addition to their area. There was a scheme for a theatre at Craven Park; another in Acton Lane (where the Crown Court was later built); and one at the corner of Harlesden High Street and Furness Road which was for the Willesden Theatre and Assembly Rooms, designed by Mr Robert F. Hodges FRIBA. It was proudly announced in *The Willesden Chronicle* in 1903 as about to go before the council's planning committee. It got no further.

It was left to the great theatre architect, Frank Matcham (1854-1920) to provide Harlesden with the district's only purpose-built theatre in the High Street. (I give great credit to the Tricycle

theatre, which remains Brent's only playhouse but its actual building is an adaptation from the Foresters' Hall, even though the stage and auditorium were their own creation). Matcham was responsible for building or renovating over eighty theatres across the British Isles; these included the Tower Ballroom and Circus at Blackpool, the Metropolitan Theatre in Edgware Road and the London Palladium.

A company led by (Sir) Walter Gibbons went ahead and speedily had the construction finished with its 3,000 seats, ready for its opening on 16 September 1907. Gibbons was born in 1871 and, after working in the early days of film-making, developed an interest in music-hall. After Willesden Hippodrome, his greatest venture was the London Palladium – the link between Gibbons and Matcham is obvious.

Bert Hammond was appointed manager and he organised the grand opening. Top of the bill was Alec Hurley, the husband of Marie Lloyd and then at the height of his fame. She came to the theatre a little later on and then many times until her untimely death in 1922. His show was called *The Costers' Beano* and described as 'his greatest and most beautiful production' – but then they all say that about themselves. The orchestra was conducted by a scion of the ducal house of Parma in Italy, Prince Robert de Broglie, while his wife, Princess Estelle, sang 'Let me Dream Again'.

From this illustrious opening, the 'Hipp' progressed well, attracting many of the top music-hall performers of the day. Sir George Robey ('the Prime Minister of Mirth' as he was called) was a frequent visitor; Violet Lorraine the singer and more comedians, Sir Harry Lauder and Harry Tate were all on the bill at one time or another. A young 'star comedienne' named Ena Dayne played there in February 1912 as well as many other lesser-known stars of the Edwardian music-hall. In April 1910, a young man named Stan Jefferson was part of the troupe, Fred Karno's Army – an immensely popular act – just before they went off to tour America. Jefferson stayed there

Opposite: Willesden Hippodrome in all its glory, 1911.

Right: (Lord) Sidney Bernstein – who revived the 'Hipp' and later created Granada Television. (Courtesy Granada Television)

and became famous as Stan Laurel of Laurel and Hardy. Plays were also on the bill – one of these, in 1911, was *The Girl Who Took the Wrong Turning* written and produced by Walter Melville (1875-1937), who was well known at that time for his many 'Bad Women' dramas.

A varied programme of cinema, music-hall and stage shows made the Hipp a very popular attraction in Willesden before the First World War. However, in the 1920s, it went through a bad patch until rescued by Sidney Bernstein who took it over and converted it into a cinema with the familiar pattern of two films and a stage show. The opening ceremony of the revitalised Hipp was on 12 September 1927 with a ceremony presided over by the Middlesex County Council chairman, Col. Charles Pinkham and presented by the most famous British female film star of the day – Miss Betty Balfour. Many of her films were made 'round the corner' in Craven Park by Pearson-Elder – and a scene from one of her films was taken at the front door of the Hippodrome, as she described it in her speech. Lord Bernstein, who was born in Ilford, East London in 1899, had gone into the film world and an early acquisition of his, just before he took over the Hippodrome, was the cinema in Church End, later given his chosen title, from his love of all things Spanish, 'The Granada'. Bernstein, who became a millionaire and who was also a socialist, extended his interest in the entertainment world to television where the name Granada was again used to great effect. He died in 1993.

Some of the shows that followed in the 1930s were grand opera (yes! In Willesden) – *The Tales of Hoffman, Madame Butterfly* and *La Bohème* – these might be followed the succeeding week by 'Circus Parade', or an Ice Spectacular, St Moritz. These were presented by the impresario Prince Littler and that would be followed by jazz, by artists including Nat Gonella and his Georgians (I met Nat during the war at a transit camp, in Italy).

However, when war came, all was not well and in September 1940 it closed for a time, as a safety measure. War made that permanent a few weeks later when a bomb, probably intended for

Willesden Junction, demolished a large part of the building. It never recovered from this disaster, although some use was made of what was left for warehousing from 1949 for a few years.

Eventually a decision was made to demolish the partial ruin. A local firm came in and built an office block, speculatively. A government department found a use for it and it has been in use for public purposes ever since. It was not quite a time to say 'hipp, hipp, hurray', but with changing times that is probably the best of uses for all. As Marie Lloyd used to sing, 'a little of what you fancy does you good'!

three

Looking at Old Brent

A Tale of Two Hospitals

Before the National Health Service came into being, hospitals were usually provided by private patrons, whether the church or wealthy philanthropic benefactors. Famous London hospitals like St Bartholomew's (Bart's), Guys or the Middlesex came about through the creation of such humanitarian foundations.

Thus it came about that the Copland sisters, Frances and especially Anne, were among the earliest and most generous of Wembley's donors. As described on page 77, they built Wembley's Parish church, St John the Evangelist, also a school, and a workmen's hall. A hospital was yet one more of their gifts to the community, endowed by Anne with £3,500 – a largish sum in 1871.

It was quite a small institution, situated just to the south of Wembley High Road, roughly where Rosemead Avenue is now and bore the name of Copland Sudbury Village Hospital, a title that tells a lot about the nature of the district at that time. A board of trustees was set up to manage the hospital and they included many of the worthies of the village, including the vicar, Revd A.C. Layard, Revd William Gray from Wembley Manor (or Wembley Park as it was known), Major General Crawford (who was soon to add the name Copland to make a hyphenated surname), Col. Sir Patrick Talbot of Oakington Farm, Thomas Sneezum, one of the richer farmers in Wembley – he held John Lyon's old farm at Preston – and William (later Sir) Perkin, the renowned chemist, who lived at Sudbury Green.

Despite this band of Wembley stalwarts, it was Anne Copland's vision which drove the hospital on, even after her death in 1872, as she left money tied up financially, and arranged for the poor to have access to the dispensary by way of a scheme of payments. Unfortunately, the investments did not quite succeed in making enough to underpin the resources of the hospital and in 1885 it closed, except for the dispensary. Mr C.D. Woolley, of High Lea, up on Wembley Hill, became its secretary. Dr Charles Goddard, who later became Wembley District Council's first Medical Officer of Health, became its medical supervisor, with new trustees including Revd John Silvester and Major R.K. Carlyon (whose name is retained in Carlyon Road, Alperton).

Eventually – I am not quite sure when – the dispensary also folded up and Dr Goddard moved in, before building his own home, Harrowdene House into which he moved in 1895. The building, which became known as 'Elmwood', was then occupied by the builder J.W. Comben (of Comben and Wakeling) and the site was sold in 1928 for redevelopment as the Majestic Cinema.

Thus it was, in the 1920s another group of the important citizens of the fast-growing Wembley, urged on by a report from the local Medical Officer of Health, realised that a hospital was now an urgent necessity. George Barham, the most eminent of them, provided a site on his family's dairy farm, off the Harrow Road, and added a donation of £1,000. His example was followed

Above: Nurses at Wembley Hospital, 1928.

Opposite above: Wembley Hospital Board of Management, *c.* 1932.

Opposite below: Duke and Duchess of York (later King George VI and Queen Elizabeth) and Princess Elizabeth, 1927.

by other gifts and this enabled the sponsors (who elected Mr Barham as president of the board) to feel confident to go ahead with the building of the hospital. The architect appointed, Harry Kenchington, was a former Wembley councillor, known to many of the trustees. On 30 October 1926, at the invitation of the trustees, the president of the Royal College of Surgeons, the distinguished Sir John Rose Bradford, laid the foundation stone.

The construction work went ahead and on 2 June 1928, it was ready to be opened by the Duke and Duchess of York – later to become King George VI and Queen Elizabeth – who was to become the Queen Mother. It had a handsome frontage, to which a small colonnade was added later. There were four, and later six, wards, with other facilities including an accident and emergency centre. It was the closure of this local asset in the 1970s which sparked a wave of resentment for a while. However, it came to be realised that the NHS, which was now in control, required better provision in larger units. Wembley reverted to a cottage-type hospital, until it was, once again, overtaken by events. The old building of 1928 is now a shadow of its former much-loved self, while a new Care Centre, which received much critical acclaim for its design, took over in the large grounds, which George Barham had so generously provided many years earlier.

Over many years, many of us have known the hospital with a mixture of happiness and sadness – the emotions always associated with such an institution. What I think made it special was the loving care its staff bestowed on the patients who came there. The receptionists, at outpatients, made you welcome, the nurses showered attention and the cleaners did their job. It was a good example of a local hospital and even though these qualities are surely found among the staff in the larger district hospitals of today's NHS, they were the essence of Wembley's own hospital.

E OLD FLOUR MILL. SHOOT-UP-HILL. 1890.

The Miller's Tale

For those of you with a literary turn of mind, I have to disappoint you, since this is nothing to do with Chaucer or *The Canterbury Tales*. Yet, this is very much to do with the way in which mills used to be part of our everyday lives from ancient times, at least until the nineteenth century.

If you have ever visited a mill, though there are few enough nowadays even as monuments to the past, you will readily understand that they involve quite complicated pieces of machinery. There is the mechanism which provides the energy – a windmill or water wheel. This movement has to be transmitted to the operation of the millstones. Finally, the ground flour has to be fed in to sacks for distribution and sale or use by the miller in baking bread.

The records of our local history tell us about only five or six mills in the area, for certain. I find this quite strange, since milling was an essential though specialised element of village life. Domesday Book – that great record of our country's worth at the time of William the Conqueror – reveals only one mill in the area and that was in Kingsbury. I believe this might have been a watermill on the river Brent. I also suggest that it was located at or near the crossing of the river at Neasden Lane – needless to say there was no Welsh Harp then, so the river wound its way down the valley between the high hills of Neasden on its southern side and Wakeman's Hill on the north. It was only a small mill, worth three shillings, but it would have been enough to serve the small population of the area.

According to the indispensable *Victoria County History of Middlesex*, there was probably a watermill further down the Brent in Willesden, which formed part of a grant made in 1325 by Richard of Cornhill (what an appropriate name) to the vicar of the parish.

Above: The Mapesbury Windmill, 1860.

Opposite above: The old steam flour mill on Shoot-up-Hill, in ruins, 1890.

There were several windmills at one or another site – for example one at about the same time as the watermill was north of the Sherrick brook, which might have been up on Dollis Hill. Sir Francis Roberts of Neasden leased a farm to William Grey in 1616 and he built a windmill on Dudden Hill Lane (which is shown on Isaac Messider's 1749 map of Willesden). It went through quite a few different owners over the next two centuries until it was pulled down. It seems a shame; it could well have served the students at the Technical College which was built nearby in 1934!

The most famous of all, was the Mapesbury, or Kilburn, windmill which has left its mark in Mill Lane, though that road is actually in Hampstead. If you look at the picture, you will see why it is of a type called a smock mill, as the shape, with sloping sides, looks something like the overall worn by country farm workers. It stood on the top of Shoot-up-Hill, well-placed to gain the maximum wind. It was on the land of the Mapesbury Manor and was built by a tenant, Isaac Ennos, in the last decade of the eighteenth century. He became quite well established in the district, owning fields and other land nearby in Hampstead. The mill certainly prospered and his daughter, Rebecca, married William Hale who took over the running of the mill in 1829.

The business continued to thrive – it would have done, given the steadily improving wealth of the district, as the Edgware Road carried more and more traffic in and out of London, with a corresponding demand for inns and hotels. There was also the strength of the farming industry on the edge of the expanding metropolis of London, with farm workers looking for their loaves of bread. Ennos and Hale were on to a good thing indeed. By 1851, as the census shows, they were employing five men at the mill and were able to build a steam mill alongside the older windmill, in 1859.

Then – disaster! William's son, Charles, had taken over the mill (although he could not have foreseen what was to happen). In December 1863, just before Christmas, gales were blowing creating havoc all round England. It seems that the wind blew so strongly, forcing the sails round so fast that it caused them to burst into flame – like a giant Catherine wheel, it was said. There was no fire brigade near enough to help deal with the blaze, which caused considerable damage to the mill and the house. Indeed, the lack of this vital facility led to the formation of the Kilburn Volunteer Fire Brigade, which thereafter did sterling work in the district.

Charles Hale continued to use the steam mill, leaving the old windmill to go to rack and ruin. However, it may be that this had taken the wind out of his sails (if you will pardon the pun) as within a few years he had sold it to the Kilburn Flour Mills operated by R. and A. Bates who kept it going for another thirty years, and then at the very end of the nineteenth century, a hundred years of Kilburn milling ended when the steam mill was demolished.

Houses were built on the site and then, in the 1960s a series of tall blocks of flats were erected by Willesden Council – one of them being called, naturally, Windmill Court.

Our Straight Roman Road

I have been fascinated by Watling Street for years. Our Kilburn High Road and Cricklewood Broadway are two of the names which we now use for this ancient highway. Now, come with me in your imagination – or go down there for real – to the corner of the High Road and Cavendish Road, outside the North London pub. Look north towards Kilburn Station. Despite the Metropolitan railway bridges, you get a clear impression of how straight the road is. Now, turn round and look towards London: again, there is that direct line determinedly moving forward to its destination.

It is this apparently undeviating construction which makes Roman roads a byword for directness. The length of our section, from Kilburn Bridge to Colindale (where it has become the Edgware Road) reveals this quite clearly. Even so, the Roman engineers were not afraid to divert where the nature of the land made it easier. At the very southern edge of the borough (as it was before boundary changes), where the old tollgate used to be, there is a kink in the road as they negotiated the old Kilburn stream (long before the culvert was built). There is another, just beyond the edge of Brent, up the top of Brockley Hill (called by the Romans *Sulloniacea*), showing how flexible those Imperial soldiers could be.

This road, the first the Romans built after they had invaded in AD43, became one of the four 'King's Highways' and remained the basis of our network. At some point, this Roman road acquired its Saxon name derived from the clan name of the *Waeclinga* the Old English name for *Verulamium* or St Albans - this later became *Waetlinga*. Chaucer, in his poem *The House of Fame*, describes the Milky Way as being like Watling Street. It became, for a short while, the boundary between King Alfred's Wessex and the Danish kingdom, the Danelaw. Then it became – as it still is – the boundary between parishes, with Willesden on the west side and Hampstead and others on the eastern border. This was lovingly described in the Willesden History Society's Millennium booklet 'Beating the Bounds'.

As the road became a main route, first soldiers, then settlers and then merchants used it for their journeys. They all needed to stop for a rest and refreshment and inns were opened to meet the need. Where the earliest ones might have been we really do not know but, by the fifteenth century, a number proudly claim to have been open for trade. There is the Cock Inn, opposite Quex Road and the Bell – actually on the Hampstead side near Kilburn High Road Station, a very good landmark. Nearby, was the Kilburn Priory, a retreat for nuns who, as part of their dedication to the service of humanity, offered food and a bed to weary travellers.

Kilburn High Road, part of Watling Street, near Quex Road, *c.* 1895. B.B. Evans' shop is prominent on the right.

High Road Brondesbury looking straight up Shoot-up-Hill as the later railway bridges were not yet obstructing the view.

'On the Edgware Road', a print by J.C. Ibbetson, c. 1790.

The Romans did not stray far from the main road; there is little evidence of their activity although remains of a possible farmhouse were discovered by the Museum of London recently at Brook Road, Neasden, a few hundred yards away from the main road. When the Anglo-Saxons moved in, they gradually settled down in farms, hamlets and then villages. These became the nuclei of the settlements which grew into modern areas like Kilburn and Cricklewood (and of course, Harlesden, Neasden, Wembley and Kingsbury).

It took the building of the railway to open up Kilburn to development. Where the railway crossed under the old Roman road, and near the bridge over the Kilburn stream, houses, shops, villas and small industries sprang up. Willesden was opening its eyes after its centuries' old slumber. Farm cottages were swept away, farms themselves melted under bricks and mortar as the unstoppable progress of modern suburbia stamped its image on acre after acre of (literally) green fields.

From the time in the 1880s when Kilburn High Road took on the shape of a Victorian shopping centre, its appearance has changed remarkably little. I have a photograph, in my book on Brent, of the High Road taken in 1898 and if anyone living at that time could look at the scene today, they would be surprised how little it has changed. Of course the shops and their frontages are different; there are no horse buses and telegraph posts have gone underground. Now there is no St Paul's church at Kilburn Square – instead there are flats and a market. The tower of the Gaumont State dominates the middle distance skyline but the essence is still there: Watling Street forever.

William IV pub on Harrow Road at Kensal Green, at the junction with Warfield Road, named after a well-known nineteenth-century landlord.

The Rise of Kensal Green

Kensal shares with Kingsbury a little royal mystery. The records show that its original name was *Kingsholte* or King's Wood. In neither case do we really know which king is meant, or even if the name was based on a particular monarch. The name first appears in 1253 which was in the middle of the long reign of Henry III – but the name may well have existed long before he even came to the throne. It may have meant no more than today naming a pub 'The King's Arms'.

Kensal has a much longer history as part of one of the ten 'Prebendal Manors', namely Chamberlayne Wood. These manors, created in 1150, were the original holdings of the Dean and Chapter of St Paul's and this tenure goes back to at least AD 938, when King Alfred's grandson, Athelstan was on the throne. In Saxon times, the churches, especially the greatest like Westminster Abbey, Canterbury Cathedral and St Paul's, had acquired large tracts of land in different parts of the country.

St Paul's allocated their lands in Willesden to ten of their prebendaries. These were religious officials of the Church who usually had no connection with the district concerned. They had stalls in the main part of the cathedral, where they would attend on High Holy Days, and which you can see today with the names of the manors painted over the top.

Thus we have the charming picture of two small woods, Kensal and Chamberlain, in this southern part of Willesden; one named for a king and the other for one of his court officers. Apart from these woods, the area was farmland, at the edge of which passed the badly-kept road from London through Paddington Willesden and Wembley on its way to Harrow – in other words, the Harrow Road.

On 25 September 1905, parents, mainly mothers, wait at the gate of Harvist Road Junior School (now Kensal Rise School) in Chamberlayne Wood Road.

In the fifteenth century, All Souls College, Oxford, (founded by Thomas Chichele, Archbishop of Canterbury) bought very large areas of the farmlands in Willesden and in Kingsbury. In further land sales, farms near to the All Souls holdings in Kensal went to Peter Maloure (or Malorees) who was what was called the 'Justiciar' (or chief-justice) of Edward I. The names in this paragraph will recognised as modern names used in the borough; All Souls Avenue, Chichele Road and Malorees Schools.

One of the famous writers of the nineteenth century came to live in Kensal Manor, on the Harrow Road. This was Harrison Ainsworth, a friend of Dickens, Thackeray and many other authors of that period, who frequently visited him at his Willesden home. Ainsworth specialised in historical romances and did a lot of research to ensure his stories were factually correct. He paints a picture of the Kensal Green of the seventeenth century in his delightful novel *Old St Paul's*.

It deals with the plague year of 1665, describing the fate of a family who leave the city to escape the horrors of this epidemic. They travel out along the Harrow Road, through the small village of Paddington, and reach a farmhouse on the summit of the hill rising from Kensal Green. The green really existed then, not large, but a typical village centre. The farmhouse where they took refuge was owned by Mr Wingfield (a name Ainsworth found in the churchyard of St Mary's Willesden). He describes the scene:

A pleasant walk across the fields brought them to the pretty village of Willesden and its old and beautiful church. They proceeded to the grave of poor Sarah Wingfield [the farmer's daughter who had just died of a broken heart] which lay at the east of the church beneath one of the tall elms.

(But do not go to look for the setting of his narrative – it is only a story, like Ainsworth's account of the burial of the highwayman Jack Sheppard in Willesden, which thousands believed to be true!)

Kensal Green remained for many years, like most of Willesden parish, a quiet rural area, on the edge of London, but not part of the Metropolis. The great cemetery which bears its name was opened in 1833, though it is actually in the Kensington Borough and this led to some modest developments, mainly for cemetery workers' houses, but also some charming villas along the Harrow Road, facing the wall.

Roads like Hazel and Purves were named respectively from the land agent for All Souls College and the solicitor of the United Land Company, which did the building work – Wakeman was the farmer who sold out to enable the developments to begin. Thus are those long-forgotten contributors to our distant past still remembered. Victor and Napier refer to the general who won a famous battle in India in 1880, though perhaps that is a little indelicate to mention today!

The coming of the London and Birmingham Railway (see p.25-27) and of the North London Line stimulated development gradually, but inevitably, up the hill from Kensal Green and the Harrow Road – and Kensal Rise was born. Among the developers were builders like Charles Langler (Langler Road) and Charles Pinkham – later a local councillor.

Kensal Manor House at 725 Harrow Road, home of Harrison Ainsworth for many years. It was later a doctor's residence and has now been demolished.

Before the houses overwhelmed the district, a National Athletics Ground was laid out in 1890 in the fields just north of Kensal Rise Station, where are now Clifford, Leigh and Whitmore Gardens. Queen's Park Rangers Football Club had been formed in that part of Queen's Park which is also known as West Kilburn. It had quite a number of bases in its early years and this athletics ground was one of them.

As Kensal developed it included the necessary features of a good town. Shops punctuated Chamberlayne Road (built by All Souls College on the line of an existing footpath to facilitate the developments) up to Kensal Rise Station. Churches were always an early mark of the parish; St John's is at the corner of the Harrow Road and Kilburn Lane, actually in Paddington but serving the whole community. When Mortimer Road was built (its eastern half later renamed Harvist Road) the Ecclesiastical Commissioners left space and from St John's the Christ Church mission was set up there but the name was later changed to St Martin. St Lawrence in Chevening Road and St Anne's in Salusbury Road – the two were later amalgamated on the latter's site and were, with St Martin, all built by the brothers Cutts.

Schools were at first provided by the Church of England, some of which have not lasted like St John's at Kensal Green. More successful were Keble Memorial in Crownhill Road, Harlesden and Princess Frederica in Purves Road – both sponsored by Emily Ayckboum.

All in all, Kensal carries a lot of history in its small, compact area.

Happy Days in Harlesden

You probably know, if you come to think about it, that Harlesden like most of the other Brent and Harrow villages can trace its origin back to Saxon times. In the 'heart of Harlesden' today there is no sign of Herewulf, the local tribal leader who set up his *tun* or farm here some twelve hundred years ago. 'Herewulf's tun' has now become the modern Harlesden.

By the time of Domesday Book, the survey completed for William the Conqueror in 1087, it had become written as *Herulvestune* and was one of the manors under the jurisdiction of St Paul's Cathedral. The tiny village (it had twenty-two householders or villagers) settled down for the next seven centuries as a peaceful place within the parish of Willesden.

By the time the famous map-maker John Rocque drew his map of London and the surrounding districts, between 1741 and 1745 as he tells us, he found it was called 'Holsdon'. He shows houses and farms mainly around the green which stretched from today's Royal Oak Inn to the Crown, along the High Street as it now is.

The coming, firstly of the Paddington (Grand Union) Canal at the end of the eighteenth century and then of the railway from Euston to Birmingham in 1837 began the transformation of the district from being a rural backwater to an industrial suburb. The genial general manager of the London and Birmingham Railway (later the London and North Western Railway), Capt. Mark Huish moved into Harlesden House and soon became quite an acceptable member of the local community. He allegedly had a station conveniently built down Acton Lane to enable him to get to his office at Euston every day!

On the Harrow Road to the east of the village was a tollgate, though this was removed in 1872. The road, going on towards its named destination, crossed the railway close to Willesden Station which had opened in 1866. That soon attracted such a radial variety of railway branches that the name Junction became highly apt. It then passed the Tubbs estate, which was at the time still fields, and reached Harlesden Green near the manor house, soon to be acquired by the Beeson family, who also took over the Crown Inn, with its pond and skittle ground, from Mr Clary.

High Street Harlesden is one of the most photographed in the Brent Archives, with the Jubilee Clock (1887), appearing in many of images of the street. This one is from 1920 – the Methodist church spire looms on the left, before it was destroyed in the Second World War.

Around 1855, there was a cluster of shops serving the local farmers, like William Sellons and James Wright, and the farm workers: a smith and farrier, a wheelwright, grocer, baker, butcher, boot maker, seedsman and florist. And then there were the inns: the Royal Oak, the Crown and the Green Man. A coach from Harrow into London called at the Crown daily, out and back, while an omnibus started from the Royal Oak at 11, 2, 4 and 7 going into town via Kensal Green. Nearby was Roundwood House, the home of Lord Brudenell and soon to become famous as the home of George Furness who did so much for Willesden (see p.14).

In 1867, a corrugated-iron-roofed building signified the arrival of a daughter church to St Mary's, to be named All Souls' when it was fully built. The new church in 1879, with its octagonal shape, was later joined by the ever-present memorial to Queen Victoria. The Jubilee Clock was erected by the council engineer, the redoubtable O. Claude Robson, in 1887 at a cost (mainly borne by public subscription) of £229 10s 6d, not including the cost of lighting and of a drinking fountain (no longer there). The shopping centre was becoming a little more like the bustling place we know today with a great variety of trades now represented, serving a population of about three thousand.

The High Street, looking east towards the Royal Oak.

'The Willows' – prominent at the corner of Park Parade (Harlesden Road) and Rucklidge Avenue; later demolished to make way for the Borough of Willesden Social Club.

At the far end of Rucklidge Avenue, Nos 154 and 156, there was, for a few years at the very end of the nineteenth century, the 'Royal Hygienic Hospital' set up by Dr Thomas Allinson (1858-1918) – it was a nursing home based on the values of 'natural living' as he described his philosophy. On more practical lines, he developed a form of wholemeal bread, which is still on sale today. At the corner of Rucklidge Avenue and what is now Park Parade (then Harlesden Road) was a fine villa, 'The Willows' (pulled down in 1914 to make way for a council fire station). It was at that time owned by one of the Wright family, Robert (a keen angler and a High Bailiff at the Bloomsbury County Court – others in his family were associated with the legal profession, as were the Sellons). John Wright lived at Sellons Farm, having taken it over from the family; Richard Wright was at 'Springwell' and James in a fine house with a lovely garden hence the road: Harlesden Gardens. Other street names today can be identified from some of these houses.

By 1910, the z-shape of the High Street was full of shops, many of which lasted well through the twentieth century – Karl Schworrer the jeweller, Penn Craft the florist, Strange and Chitham outfitters, Claude Bastable builder, Hedley Molyneux stationers, Beeson Brothers hardware and Horace Borer outfitter. What a wonderful parade of names and what service they provided. Today's shops can just as well be said to serve the vastly changed population of Harlesden, so that it can truly be said that little alters in Harlesden, least of all the spirit of its residents. It is now a miniature United Nations of people, who surely relish the connection with the ancient Saxons who gave the area its name.

A class at Pound Lane Infants' School, 1932.

Sellon's Farm – one of several in Harlesden which surrounded the Green.

Farm cottages in Harlesden Road in 1904.

The Rising Sun Inn on Harlesden Road, 1893 – then a typical country pub.

The Welsh Harp

Come on – do you really know why the Welsh Harp was originally built? As a drinking water reservoir? As a boating lake? To preserve fish supplies? For irrigation?

It has been used for some of these (but not for drinking water, please) but it goes back to the days of the canal boom. The Grand Junction Canal had been built in from London (Brentford) to Birmingham and in 1801 added the Paddington Branch, to bring the narrow boats into the heart of London. It passed through Wembley – at Alperton – and Harlesden on its way to join the Regents Canal to Camden, Islington and Stepney.

Canals need a water supply and it was soon realised that more would be needed (the Ruislip Reservoir, now the Lido, proved to be insufficient). The river Brent was seen as the most likely source – thus a feeder was built in 1810. It is still there and can be seen in different parts of its journey; it flows round the back of Gibbons Recreation Ground, under Twybridge Way and then shortly goes under the wide expanse of railway lines before reaching the canal itself near Waxlow Road.

However, this still turned out to provide an insufficient supply for the busy canal and it was decided to build a reservoir. To do this, the river Brent was dammed at Neasden, thus flooding the valley at the foot of Dollis Hill, where the Dollis brook and the Silk stream fed the Brent itself. The original river line still forms the boundary between Brent and Barnet, at this point, even though it is actually under water! The reservoir was built between 1833 and 1835. Sadly, tragedy struck before it was finished, when three Sidebottom brothers, from Mount Pleasant at Roe Green, died while bathing; their elder brother was also drowned, heroically, though unsuccessfully, trying to save them.

Possibly named from the Brent reservoir (or maybe the other way round!), the Old Welsh Harp, seen here in 1880, was run by William Warner and known as 'the jolliest place that's out'.

Sailing on the Welsh Harp – the canal storage reservoir is an ideal base for yachting.

After it was finished, another disaster followed, though this time without loss of life. In November 1840, the fields from Kingsbury to Stonebridge lay under water after torrential rain (so what's new?). As Simeon Potter puts it:

> When Sunday came, the sweet chime of bells [of Kingsbury church] could not be heard beyond the limits of the churchyard, so deafening was the sound made by the torrent of water as it tumbled over the floodgate. Still the rain continued. The worst was to follow. On the night of 16 January 1841, the dam burst and the waters swept onwards unimpeded. It was sink or swim for every creature caught that night in the oncoming flood.

There is no record of anyone being hurt nor was there any serious damage to property in Brent itself, but there was severe flooding down at Brentford.

In more recent times, the river Brent has been culverted and channelled where once it was a sweetly-flowing stream, bordered by trees and supporting many fish for the willing angler to seek. With the phenomenal spread of railways in the mid-nineteenth century, the canals slowly died a lingering death (although they are, thankfully, still hanging on today). Other uses have been found for the Welsh Harp.

The shape of the reservoir is unmistakably like a harp, but it probably gets its nickname from the inn that used to stand on the Edgware Road, the Old Welsh Harp. I have a theory that this name was encouraged by William Warner, the best-known member of the family which owned that pub in the nineteenth century. It was known to Victorians by repute and by song as 'the jolliest place that's out' (you should hear the Kingsbury Amateur Dramatic Society, including the well-known Kingsbury historian, Geoff Hewlett, singing the song for all they're worth). The inn – which goes back at least to the eighteenth century, one of a number serving travellers on Watling Street – was rebuilt in 1859 and, until 1889, was run and popularised by William Perkins Warner, a Crimean War veteran and son of the owner of Blackbird Farm at Neasden.

Warner offered boating, fishing, tea gardens, indoor sports, a concert hall and a museum of fish and animals caught in the vicinity. In 1870, the Midland Railway opened the Welsh Harp Station especially to serve this pleasure resort which attracted 'hordes of beanfeasters with merry song [...] of cornets and concertinas'. Warner also set up and ran the Kingsbury Racecourse on the lower slopes of Barn Hill and then moved it behind the public house until it was suppressed by an Act of Parliament forbidding racecourses within twelve miles of London, as a carnival of vice! The first mechanical hare was tried out in a greyhound race run here, *The London Encyclopaedia* tells us.

Part of the eastern end was filled in and factories built there. The southern side has some factories bordering the North Circular Road, but most of this part is a recreation ground where sunbathing, believe it or not, was objected to by local residents. On this stretch of water, an annual regatta was held first by Willesden and then by Brent Council. Supported by the sailing clubs, who began in the 1930s and which have their bases on the north side, this was a very popular outing. The councillors challenged a team from other boroughs to a rowing race, white-sailed boats skimmed in pursuit of each other over the still water, canoeing and other water sports added to an exciting day as the author well remembers as Mayor of Brent – and would love to see it revived. It is also a marvellous place to study bird life (undisturbed by the boating activities) and aquatic flora. At one time, a floating raft was constructed at the eastern end, anchored with a long hawser, on which a family of grebes built their nest, safe from visitors.

In that same year, the author attended the opening of the Staples Corner flyover (the one which Republican bombers had a go at a few years ago). This was part of a massive road construction project which included the demolition of the Old Welsh Harp inn and when it was all over, they found the space was not really needed after all.

Postcard showing River Brent from Kingsbury Bridge, now Blackbird Hill.

The northern bank is mostly in Barnet, with the twisty Cool Oak Lane paralleling the edge. On the Brent part, the council set up the Welsh Harp Environmental Education Centre – a long name for a remarkably clever unit for helping town-bred children get close to understanding nature. Next door was the seed-bed for Brent's famous parks, Chilcott Nursery, named after the one-time Council Parks Officer (see p.18); it is now a well-organised commercial garden nursery, 'Greenhouse'.

The Welsh Harp remains a place of tranquillity, even though it is only a few yards from the busy North Circular Road. In winter it may be a little bleak, but on a sunny summer afternoon, it is again 'the jolliest place that's out'.

Here Lies ... Wild Flowers, Bats and Ferns

If you talk to friends about open spaces in the locality, you would discuss Fryent Open Space, or one of the parks such as Roundwood, Barham or Queen's. We should not overlook, as the organisation English Nature has pointed out, the part played by cemeteries, churchyards and burial grounds in providing support for wildlife in our cities.

You have only to think of the three original parish churches and their burial sites at St Mary's Willesden, Old St Andrew's in Kingsbury and St John's, Wembley (the 'newest' of the three, but still one hundred and fifty years old) and you can imagine yourself under a tree in a corner of any one of these, observing the flowers and the creatures that flourish there. You feel close to nature, and this is due not only to the calming and easeful atmosphere but also to the sense of sanctity and solitude that demonstrably surrounds these havens of rest.

The ways in which we dispose of our dead have been identified since earliest times – part of the variety of burial customs over many millennia. Pyramids for Pharaohs or barrows for the elite of British tribes or cremation in other times and climes. Christian burial in consecrated ground became customary in Britain as the religion became established in Saxon Britain after the Romans had left.

Burials have taken place at St Mary's in Willesden probably since the tenth century and certainly since the thirteenth, though the earliest remains are no longer traceable. While inside are brasses, wall monuments and ledger stones to the former notable families of the parish – the Roberts, the Franklyns, Wrights and Finches – outside, open to the sky, the rain, the sun and the stars, there among the trees are more tombs for the past eminent citizens and some more recent: George Furness and his family, Charles Reade the novelist and F.A. Wood the local historian. However, here does not lie the highwayman, Jack Sheppard. The great Victorian novelist, Harrison Ainsworth, invented his story, including a fictional relationship with Willesden, although many people, at the time believed his writing and came to St Mary's to see for themselves. Ainsworth is himself buried at Kensal Green Cemetery.

At Old St Andrews, even though the church itself is closed through dilapidation, the grounds are alive with natural life: wild flowers of all descriptions, bird life and small animals. They roam among the standing monuments (some, as in too many churchyards, vandalised by thoughtless and ignorant idiots) close to Old Church Lane, one leg of which was sensibly closed off by the council. Inside among the brasses is one to a certain John Bul who died in 1621 and may possibly be the original for our stout John Bull.

St John's Wembley, while so much newer, relatively, has its share of worthies buried in the old burial ground, which was taken over by the Wembley Burial Board 'at Harrow' in 1887. It is a good example today of a parish church and ground close to a busy High Street but quiet even a few yards away from the rush of traffic. In its grounds, the benefactors of the church, the Copland sisters (another of their useful local benefactions) had a small schoolhouse built in 1849; it continued until the school at Alperton was built and opened in 1879 and then was used only as a Sunday school. The buildings remained until as late as 1972.

One surprise is the cemetery in Willesden Lane. The author used to look out of a window at Kilburn Grammar School, (when the teacher was not watching!) into this old cemetery and its chapels: an oasis of green in the urban scene. It was known as the Paddington Old Cemetery (built in 1855) and was owned by Westminster Council who owned three others. They decided to rid themselves of this municipal facility. What happened to three of them is a scandal told elsewhere, but in the case of Paddington, it was a model of inter-council co-operation. Brent took it over in 1985 (for one pound) and set about its policy of creating a lawn cemetery. Brent's residents and plot-holders benefited. The London Wildlife Trust worked with the council to uphold a country atmosphere – planting bushes, installing nest boxes and grassing areas, where suitable. Among those buried here are the late Cllr Peter Pendsay (Mayor of Brent 1983-4), Arthur Orton, 'the Tichborne Claimant' and the Earl Mount Cashel.

Willesden's main public cemetery is the so-called 'New Cemetery' in Franklin Road (named after one of the old Willesden families), built in 1891 and opened by F.A. Wood. It had two beautiful chapels but they were regrettably demolished in 1986 by Brent Council, because of the cost of repairs. As it filled up, the council decided to create an additional burial ground and took up an option at Birchen Grove. However, hardly was it consecrated when it was realised that a site at Carpenders Park would provide a far better site for the new lawns-type cemetery. Birchen Grove became the Welsh Harp Environmental Education Centre, and the chapel is used as a classroom. Around the site, children follow a nature trail – worms instead of tombs.

Above: This 1855 print shows the chapel at Paddington Cemetery in Willesden Lane, designed by Thomas Little.

Left: Willesden's New Cemetery in Franklin Road – the chapel entrance as it was before demolition in 1936.

Wembley's own public cemetery was set up at Alperton during the First World War. It was decided by the council to try to enlarge it by purchasing the Sudbury Golf Course, but that did not succeed. They then sought to build it on the edge of the then Northwick Park golf course, but again this was frustrated in 1947 when the club closed and the site was chosen for a hospital (this became Northwick Park Hospital) and a technical college.

Described as the 'Rolls Royce among Jewish cemeteries' is the United Synagogue Cemetery in Glebe Road. Here are buried many of the famous families in the Anglo-Jewish community including many Rothschilds, Lord Bearsted, Gerald Bright (known as Geraldo, the band leader) and Lord Duveen, the art collector. Next door is the Liberal Jewish Cemetery, where my mother is buried.

A glance at a local gazetteer reveals the value to the community in terms of open space, access and freedom from modern pressures that our burial grounds, cemeteries and churchyards bring. 'The moan of doves in immemorial elms' as Tennyson put it – though he did not have to reckon with Dutch elm disease! We should be thankful for the opportunity to rest awhile in such tranquillity.

four

Lovely Old Houses

A Tale of Two Houses

Strolling through Barham Park, on the Harrow Road in Wembley, one of the most beautiful parks in north-west London, you can let your imagination people it with hundreds of guests, dressed in the best of 1920's styles, as they wandered through the attractive grounds of what was then Barham Park Mansion, invited there by George Titus Barham. It was not always like that.

Near where the Harrow Road, after passing through Wembley village, turns north towards Sudbury and Harrow, the 1746 map by John Rocque shows the Sudbury Stone – now long since moved or destroyed – and a small house. This seems to be the one belonging to the Crab family. In essence it is still here on the Harrow Road, by Barham Park, after over 250 years.

James Crab sold it to a naval man called John Copland in 1801 and thus the illustrious name comes into Wembley history. Copland was about forty years old (born around 1769, he died in 1843) and, as Dr Richard Brock – the historian of St John's church and a former head of Copland School – tells us, he had a long career as a purser in the Royal Navy (he apparently got his first posting because of his copperplate handwriting which can still be seen on documents). He retired after serving in many ships all over the world, including the West Indies and continued a profitable career as a Prize and Navy Agent.

He had married young, to Frances Trevan from Cornwall. Their five children were born there between 1787 and 1798 (I said he married young!). Sadly, one died in infancy; his son John died aged nineteen, while Eliza lived for fifty years. Anne and Frances survived, though neither married, until the 1870s. The only portrait I have seen of Anne Copland, suggests to me someone with West Indian connections, which – if correct – would make her the first lady from the Caribbean in Wembley, but this leaves the mystery of who her mother was.

After their father's death, the sisters were left a considerable fortune which they used for the benefit of their village. At first, they continued living in the building their father had acquired (and now known as Old Court). It is a delightful building and, though it has a long frontage on the Harrow Road, it is set back from the main road. The entrance to what is now the Barham Park Library must have been very gracious with gates, a drive and a timber-framed building with leaded windows. There have been some changes and additions to the structure, both inside and out, but it eventually became – and still is – a library, meeting rooms and veterans' club. John Copland also acquired, by diligent purchases, quite an extensive parkland, much of which fortunately still remains, with grassy banks, tree-shaded paths and greensward.

In this charming landscape, the sisters built their own beautiful Victorian, Gothic Mansion which they called Sudbury Lodge. It was a large house, well decorated and with delightful views across to Harrow church (there was no Chiltern Railway to block the view).

Barham Mansion, originally Sudbury Lodge, was built by the Copland sisters and then became the home of the Barham family. It was gifted to Wembley Council by Titus Barham and then pulled down in 1957 as they could no longer maintain it.

Crab's House on Harrow Road, Wembley. The original part of this building later became Barham Park. It now houses a local library, council offices and a veterans' club.

Above left: The intended Charter Mayor of Wembley in 1937, George Titus Barham, who sadly died the day the Charter was signed by the King. E.J. Butler took over as Charter Mayor.

Above right: Mrs Florence Barham.

They also used their inheritance wisely in benefactions which included the new parish church of St Johns, a schoolroom, the Workmen's Institute and a hospital. But, when first Frances and then Anne died (in 1872), the estate once more changed hands. At least, it was passed to General Robert Crawford, on condition that he took on the name of Copland – which he, obligingly, did.

It was on his death in 1895 that the Barham family came into the Wembley picture. There were Barhams in Kent in the eleventh century, taking their name from the eponymous village on Watling Street. In 1836 George Barham was born in London (a distant cousin, Richard, wrote *The Ingoldsby Legends*, one of which was the story of 'The Jackdaw of Rheims'). He became a dairyman and realised that railways provided a speedy means of bringing milk from the country, since London was growing so fast that it was eating up the dairy farms. He set up the Express Country Milk Supply Company in 1864, which was soon shortened to the familiar name Express Dairy Company. Later this company split into two – milk supply and teashops and retail. George – who was knighted in 1904 – had two sons, Arthur who took over the wholesale milk supply (which eventually became United Dairies) and George Titus, who lived in Wembley in the house his father bought from General Copland-Crawford's estate and was usually called by his middle name. He had been born with a malformation of his spine, but took great pride in horse riding, as seen when he famously led the Victory Parade through the High Road in 1919.

He bought the fields opposite the house, now renamed Barham Park Mansion, and turned them into a model Dairy Farm. When Brent Council developed them for housing after the Second World War, one of the roads was naturally called Farm Avenue. He began a lifelong interest in local affairs including a spell on Wembley District Council.

It was in this role that tragedy took place. Wembley sought borough status in 1937. On the day the charter was signed by King George in July, Titus, who would have been Charter Mayor, died.

His house and grounds and his historic collection, were bequeathed to his beloved council, to keep in trust, but within a couple of years, the war overtook any thoughts of using the house as a local centre and it was used by Civil Defence, which did not help its upkeep. After the war thoughts again turned to the idea of a civic centre but time passed and by 1954 it was estimated to cost over £16,000 to restore and convert it. As months went by, the cost rose and a stormy meeting of Wembley Council on 26 January 1956 debated its fate. Cllr Edith Lewis, member for Wembley Central, next to Barham Park angrily condemned the demolition proposal but a combination of Labour and Conservative councillors decided by thirty-one votes to fourteen that it would go. All that remains of the lovely house are the balustrade walls, but the grounds have been made into one of Brent's most delightful parks, a joy to behold and the pleasurable place in which to sit, or to stroll as you fancy takes you – and imagine the fine house that once held great parties – and Crab's House is still usefully with us.

The Story of Grove Park

If you go far enough back in the records of Kingsbury, you find a reference to the Grove family of Stanmore and Edgware who held land alongside Stag Lane, to the north of Hay Lane, in the fourteenth to fifteenth centuries. Then, as so often happened in these lush farming lands of north Middlesex, different owners appear on the documents, usually of families who leased their farms out – allowing for continuous profitable occupation. All Souls College is probably the best-known name in Kingsbury as an 'absentee landlord'.

If I jump to the 1880s, it is to avoid too much tedious detail and we then find Grove Park with a pleasant villa set in the middle of a landscaped parkland, the home to Michael Walton, until he died in 1892.

It was then that the most famous occupant of this charming home came to live in it – seemingly for the rest of his life. It was the soldier known to men who served under him as 'Bobs' and to his fellow officers as 'Kipling's General' – Field Marshal Lord Roberts of Kandahar, VC, to honour him with his full title.

He was born in 1832 in India where his father, of Irish descent, was a senior serving officer. He himself joined the Indian Army when he was twenty-one. As luck would have it, he was still quite a junior staff officer when, in 1857, the Indian Mutiny broke out. He distinguished himself to the extent that he was awarded not only several medals for courage, but the ultimate decoration, the Victoria Cross. It is one of the saddest ironies of the family that his only son Frederick Hugh was killed in South Africa and also gained the VC, posthumously.

By topical coincidence, his actual title comes from his service during the Second Afghan War, when by a further feat of great bravery he embarked on a forced march in order to raise the siege of the town of Kandahar. He remained in India, becoming commander-in-chief of the entire Indian forces (and made Baron Roberts by Queen Victoria), until he retired in 1893. This was when he found his 'home' at Grove Park. He settled in, almost as the squire of Kingsbury and became very popular in the locality. Polo games were played on the lawn of Grove Park and it became a fashionable centre. Suddenly, duty called and 'Bobs' was promoted to Field Marshal to take command in Ireland. Then, after the tragedy of his son's death in South Africa, he was sent as Commander-in-Chief to organise the Boer War. When the First World War broke out in 1914, and 'Bobs' was eighty-two years old, he offered his services but died soon after in November 1914, a hero to the end.

Right: Lord Roberts VC who lived at Grove Park Mansion in the 1890s – one of Queen Victoria's most distinguished soldiers. (Courtesy National Portrait Gallery)

Below: The East Front of Grove Park Mansion, *c.* 1900. From here Lord Roberts could look out from his bedroom window towards Hendon. (From the Walton Collection, courtesy Geoff Hewlett)

During this war, Grove Park was taken over by the Aircraft Manufacturing Company, known as Airco, who used the grounds as a landing strip and the house for offices. Housing developments encroached from the east, but the shrunken estate continued as the home for a boys' school until it closed at the outbreak of the Second World War. Sad to relate, the delightful mansion was pulled down after the war when the local authority acquired the site.

The story is not over yet! The name 'Grove Park School' was taken over for a special school for children with physical handicaps when it moved to this site in 1968. The Queen visited the school in 1990 for its Diamond Jubilee. Nearby, the council built a residential home for elderly people and, with well-deserved appropriateness, named it 'Roberts Court' (though this use has now ended). To complete the intense use the council made of this site, on the western corner was erected another special school, for children with severe learning difficulties which is now called 'Hay Lane School'.

It is one of the delights of delving into local history to find corners of our district with an almost unknown connection to the locality and then finding the links stretch in such unimagined directions – the home of a great hero, a wartime landing ground, a school and another and another – the connections with people is endless, but every one tells a story.

The Lost Manor Houses

Think of a country house and you picture an Agatha Christie play or a 1930s British film. I am being slightly unfair, but there are so few of these left in Metropolitan London today. Your imagination must bring to life the ghosts of the buildings long gone which are evoked by street names such as Manor House Drive, off Brondesbury Park, or Manor Park Road in Harlesden. Curiously, the Manor Farm Road in Alperton takes its name from a long-vanished manor farm, but it was never the focus of any manor.

As Domesday Book shows, much of Willesden was in the possession of St Paul's Cathedral and it remained like that throughout the Middle Ages and, indeed, until recent times. Names like Dean Road, Chapter Road and St Paul's Avenue, reflect the close connection. Using Willesden's apportionment into manors, the cathedral allocated a prebendary to each, with a magnificent named mahogany seat in the stalls at St Paul's. A prebendary is a priest serving the cathedral whose pay for those duties came from the land allotted to them. The manors were: The Rectory, Oxgate, Harlesden, Willesden (or Bounds), Brondesbury, Mapesbury, East Twyford, Chamberlain and Neasden – most of them still familiar local names. Just to confuse you a bit more, a large part of Mapesbury and Brondesbury was hived off to a 'sub-manor' called Malorees, which was acquired by All Souls College, Oxford, in the fifteenth century – from this we get the name of the school in Christchurch Avenue.

Even before the present long-lived building was erected, Oxgate Manor was able to claim as prebendary the famous William of Wykeham, from whom the local school takes its name. He became Bishop of Winchester and founded Winchester School and New College Oxford in the late fourteenth century. Another prebendary was Polydor Vergil, an historian and cleric in the time of Queen Elizabeth I while another two went on to become archbishops of Canterbury, no less – William Sancroft and John Tillotson. The only surviving relic of the manorial houses is the oldest secular building in Brent – the Oxgate Farmhouse – and it was not a manor house in the true sense. It stands modestly in Coles Green Road, Tudor timber-framed with its two gables facing the road. Its tiled roof is typical of its period, although its present condition is parlous and further help from the local council is needed – it might well become another of the lost manor houses. In the nineteenth century, Oxgate went to the other extreme, as you might say, when it became a centre for horses and was called Willesden Paddocks. Later, during the First World War, early tank experiments took place on the upper slopes of the Oxgate farmland. Hence Tankridge Close.

Mapesbury House – one of the oldest manor houses in Willesden (this is a nineteenth-century rebuilding) until demolished in 1925 to make way for Coverdale Road.

Harlesden Manor House – rather a grand title for a modest farmhouse, with a tall, peculiar chimney. It stood on Harlesden Green.

Oxgate Farmhouse in 1904, the oldest secular building in Willesden dating from the reign of Queen Elizabeth I – now, regrettably in a very dilapidated state.

The most majestic of the lost manors was surely at Brondesbury. Its name derives from an unknown Saxon farmer named Brand, whose name was also applied to a narrow lane shown on old maps going north and south from the manor house – Brand's Causeway. Among the people who lived there in the nineteenth century were Sir Coutts Trotter, Lady Salusbury (whose family name is recalled in Salusbury Road) and Lucy Soulsby who took over the house to be run as a girls' boarding school. She retired at the beginning of the First World War, but the school continued until 1933. The author remembers when he was a young boy, walking along Brondesbury Park, seeing the house, with its ivy-covered walls, delightful open cupola and dozens of chimneys.

Not far from there, on the other side of Willesden Lane and also vanished – when it was demolished in 1923 – was Mapesbury House, on what is now Coverdale Road. Walter Map was one of the first prebendaries appointed, in the late twelfth century, and one of the few who actually lived in 'his' manor. He gave his name to the house and to Mapes Lane (the old name for Willesden Lane, a Borough Ward and, perhaps, if residents have their way, even a tube station). He was a travelling justice for King Henry II; he was also an observer of courtly life about which he wrote a collection of witty sayings in Latin. The house he built was reconstructed in the time of Queen Anne and it was this graceful-looking house which succumbed to the pressure of post-First World War builders. During the 1860s, the once well-known novelist and journalist, Edmund Yates (for whom Yates Court in Willesden Lane is named) lived there. His greatest fame today is that he wrote an article to which Thackeray objected and had Yates thrown out of the Garrick Club! He described living in a totally rural Willesden 'a delightful place but somewhat difficult of access and not too easy to find'. A friend of his wrote to him, in January 1864:

> I started from Bayswater in a cab. I was exactly one hour and forty minutes in that cab. On our arrival in Willesden Lane I knocked and rang at three large gates, but nobody knew anything about your house. It was bitterly cold and what with anxiety and shivers, I at last was obliged to return home by Kilburn Gate.

The writer refers to the tollgate at the foot of Kilburn Bridge. Oh dear.

Willesden Manor House (the manor was also called Bounds, as it was on the parish boundary) stood on the Edgware Road between Oxford Road and Cambridge Avenue and had a very uneventful history and was, as Simeon Potter describes it, 'ignominiously pulled down in 1825'. Its sole memorial is the sign that reads 'Manor Terrace' above the row of shops fronting Kilburn High Road where it once stood.

Neasden House had a long history – once called Catwoods, it came into the control of the famous Roberts family, finishing up as a golf club house, before even this, the largest and most stately of all the Willesden manor houses was felled by the demolition men.

Harlesden Manor was also no more than a modest farmhouse, close to the green, long owned by the Finch family and later by the Beesons. East Twyford's centre was a house at Lower Place, near where the building that became Central Middlesex Hospital was erected, while West Twyford, although linked to Willesden Parish is in Greenford (now Ealing). I conclude with a reference to my favourite Victorian author (or second only to Dickens), Harrison Ainsworth. His third home in Willesden was the house of the Chamberlayne Wood Manor at Kensal Green. It backed on the 'new' All Souls' Cemetery and a picture shows a large white building with an arched colonnade on the west frontage, with a lawn on which Ainsworth walked and talked with Thackeray, Dickens and other friends.

The loss of so many lovely buildings can only be a cause for sadness and for sorrow that our predecessors had so little regard for the value of good architecture in the community. At least we can thank photographers like Henry Fisher and H. W. Reeves who recorded what we have lost for us still to relish.

Wembley Manor – Our White House

We know where Wembley Park is today. But where was the original Wembley Park? Where was the 'quiet and retired place' as it was described and what was the lavishly decorated mansion?

The story starts with one of the largest and most wealthy families of Middlesex in the Middle Ages whose strength lasted until the nineteenth century – the Pages. In 1543, as part of the process known as the Dissolution of the monasteries, the small but powerful Kilburn Priory was stripped of its holdings, which included the manor-farm at Wembley and it was granted to Richard Page, remaining in that family (the head was often called Richard) until 1803. Page also took over Uxendon Manor from the Bellamys (see p.97). It then descended through his family, although tenant farmers often occupied it and the adjoining farms called Wellers and Botnall.

Wembley Manor House, also called the White House.

In 1771, Wembley Manor came to another Richard Page, aged twenty-three, on the death of his father. He took over the farmhouse at Wellers improving it in stages. He engaged the famous landscape architect Humphrey Repton (who had worked for Lady Salusbury at Brondesbury Manor) to convert the farmland into parkland, with many trees, follies and vistas – the details of his scheme can be found in his famous 'Red Book'. After it had been completed we can imagine Page looking out of the windows of his manor house to see these engaging sights, which included looking up to Barn Hill, which was part of his estate. You can also imagine him walking to the top of Barn Hill, resting by the pond and then looking back to his house, seeing fields and woodland north and south – Wembley Hill in the distance and Harrow Hill to his right.

Sadly, he did not have very long to enjoy the fruits of his scheme as he died, childless in 1803. By his will, the estate went to his brother Francis, who died a few years later, then to his next brother William and eventually to Henry. What happened after Richard died is shrouded in mystery and would require another chapter to try to piece together but the story would include a mention of the 'Page Millions' which, if they existed, seem to have disappeared in some scandalous fashion. The Pages' solicitor seems to have become enmeshed in the sorry business – Henry Page being 'persuaded' to leave the land to him five days before his death in 1829.

Whatever the truth of all that, what does seem clear is that, about the time of Richard Page's death, a very respectable brandy merchant and governor of Harrow School, John Gray, became its owner (but not Barn Hill). Gray carried out more improvements to the house until he died in 1829. It was his son who continued the improvements which earned it its name of the 'White House'.

Thus the Revd John Gray, born in 1800, came to live there with his wife and family, enjoying his 'earthly paradise' until his own death at the advanced age of eighty-seven. His wife, Susannah, died young in 1839, perhaps worn out by having given birth to nine children who seem to have died in their infancy. Wembley Park (this one and other quotations are taken from *A History of Wembley*) was described in 1834 as 'a beautiful demesne with 272 acres of rich meadowland

The estate of Wembley Manor House, designed by the great landscape gardener Humphrey Repton and named the original Wembley Park.

and pasturage. These grasslands, including plantations, were bounded by the river Brent (seen in the distance from the house) and were beautifully diversified by fine grown timber, judiciously placed'. The annual hay harvest was gathered by Irish labourers (some of whom were recorded in the 1831 census in Wembley).

If we could still enter, it would be into a 'hall, at a small Doric portico, the door of mahogany, painted and glazed with plate glass. The hall would have been paved with Portland stone, with small diamonds of black marble, and divided from the principal staircase by a screen of scagliola [concrete and chips] columns and pilasters, in imitation of marble'. It is enough to make one weep that so-called progress permitted the destruction of so fine a world of secluded splendour.

One more description reads:

> Along the banks of the stream flowing through the park; this is the Wealdstone brook, at the back of Brook Avenue and then underground to the Brent near the stadium among the copses and osier beds can be found a mass of wild flowers, with dragon flies darting over the water and then vanishing into the deep shades of the plantations.

Such a sight would gladden the rustic heart of the most urbanised of today's citizens. Even to John Gray, born at the beginning of the century, it was evident that the world had not stood still. The tranquillity of Wembley Park was about to be shattered and Gray was shrewd enough to take advantage. The Metropolitan Railway under its thrusting chairman, Sir Edward Watkin had been planning an extension from Baker Street to Harrow (see p.13) and the land they needed would run right across his estate. He willingly sold forty-seven acres and the line was speedily extended in 1880 from Willesden Green to its new terminus. In 1889, after his death, the rest of the land was sold, also to the Metropolitan.

Watkin knew he had bought a goldmine. The first thing he did was to create a huge amusement park and called it, simply and obviously, 'Wembley Park' – with a station, opened in 1894 to serve it, very profitably. Even more was to come – the large and excessive amount of parkland was soon to become suburban housing, 'Metroland'. The manor house which became a home for French nuns for a few years was demolished in 1908. All that remains is a thatched lodge at the corner of Wembley Park Drive and Wembley Hill Road - which is now a listed building. It survived a bus crash one snowy winter evening in 1973, subsequently much restored, thanks to some help from Brent's heritage fund.

As you walk down Wembley Park Drive or the appropriately named Manor Drive, you can try to imagine the White House - and recall the elegance of the one-time 'paradise' in Wembley.

A Very Liberal House

On Dollis Hill, just below the crest of Neasden stands a now dilapidated mansion overlooking the magnificent sweep of Gladstone Park. It has been there for almost two hundred years and for much of that time it has been in and out of the news – more recently for rather sad reasons. This is Dollis Hill House, built for the Finch family in 1825. If it is more interesting for its history than for its architectural style, it is still one of the few grand buildings left in Brent – or would be if it were restored to its past glory, following two disastrous arson attacks in the late 1990s. In a magazine article of 1822, the writer described his walk through Willesden:

On Dollar's [sic] Hill, is Mr Finch's farm, which as an object from the valley below has a pleasing effect, with a view from the top as far as Leith Hill in Surrey.

Within a few years, this view was seen from the windows of Mr Finch's new house. Soon after, as these things went, it passed to Lord Tweedmouth, who as a senior member of the Liberal Party began the political connection that lasted until the end of the nineteenth century.

A little later – Victoria was now on the throne – it was bought by Lord Aberdeen and it was his son who took over the house, in 1882, with his wife Lady Ishbel. They made it the place for Liberal politicians, especially Gladstone, to stay and rest from the endeavours of parliamentary life down at Westminster. The great Liberal leader was by this time in his seventies, but 'a marvel of physical and mental vigour', as a supporter described him. He was able to use Dollis Hill House as a quiet retreat, near to Downing Street, thanks to the Aberdeens. His bedroom was on the first floor at the east end of the house, looking towards Hampstead and he worked, for the most part, on his government papers in the library which was immediately below. In the clement weather, much of his time was spent outdoors, with meals taken on the veranda (later obscured by an unsightly addition to the house). Often, there would be a gathering of politicians under the trees, some of which still frame the patio area. Trees were one of Gladstone's obsessions. Legend has it that he cut them down, in the fashion of George Washington, but the truth is that he planted many – some at Dollis Hill, including a pine tree and a fir – though I cannot vouch for them still being there.

In 1887, the Golden Jubilee of Queen Victoria was celebrated throughout the country and across the then British Empire, and the leaders of the colonies came to London to join in the festivities. Gladstone invited them up the house at Neasden and there is a picture of him, resplendent in a Derby bowler hat, with four of his colleagues, on the lawn. Others who received the invitation to call included Joseph Chamberlain, Lord Rosebery, Lord Randolph Churchill (father of Winston), the then Archbishop of Canterbury and many other men of eminence (the only woman who seems to be involved was none other than the Premier's wife – such was the political correctness of the time).

Dollis Hill House, 1908. Having been acquired by Willesden Council, it became a place for social gatherings and this tea garden was used by visitors to Gladstone Park.

Bandstand in Gladstone Park, 1905.

Lord Aberdeen was appointed Lord Lieutenant for Ireland for a short period in the 1880s and this brought him into even closer contact with Gladstone whose most difficult task was trying to bring about Home Rule for Ireland. When he was made Governor General of Canada in 1897, he gave up Dollis Hill House and it was leased to Sir Hugh Gilzean Reid. In 1900, Reid invited the famous humorist, Mark Twain, to stay with him. The writer, who was famous for his perceptive comments on the places he visited (read his *Innocents Abroad*, for instance), spoke of the delight he had in living there. 'He had,' he said, 'never seen any place that was so satisfactorily situated, with its noble trees and stretch of country, and everything that went to make life delightful, and all within a biscuit's throw of the metropolis of the world'.

Maybe these comments inspired Willesden Council to persist in their plan to buy the house and, especially, its grounds as a public park. In any event, in February 1900, the transaction was completed – at a cost of over £51,000 and, in honour of the recently deceased statesman, it was named Gladstone Park.

After that, in public ownership, the house became a tea-room and during the First World War was a hospital for wounded soldiers and after the war remained in use as a convalescent home. The council then tried to realise its potential and it became 'The Country House Restaurant'. Once Brent took over it was also used as a training centre for catering students from Kilburn Polytechnic; the local Rotary Club met there regularly. And it obtained Grade II listed status, in 1974. The stables became the Stables Art Gallery, a successful venture by devoted local painters and craftsmen and women.

In the 1990s, the House started to go downhill. Brent Council could not decide what to do with it. Arsonists tried to help by burning it – twice! It now stands, a miserable wreck of its former self awaiting a decision: to restore it as a commercial restaurant or pull it down and replace it with a park cafeteria. Local residents, up in arms, proposed a third option; to raise funds to restore it and then turn it into a community centre. It would be a shame if a building – albeit damaged – with such historical connections were to disappear. But is there a fairy godmother out there who could help with the money?

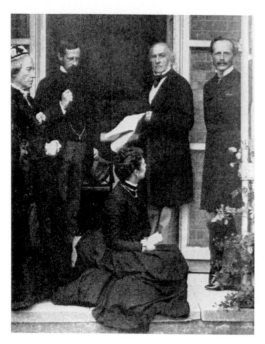

Mr Gladstone and his wife at his favourite place of leisure away from parliamentary activity with Lord and Lady Aberdeen, the owners, and Professor Drummond in about 1888.

five

How It Happened

The Hero of Stag Lane

Geoffrey de Havilland (born in July 1882 near High Wycombe) came to work at Airco in Kingsbury in April 1914. At thirty-one, he was a skilled airman and a practical aircraft designer who had begun work for the newly formed Royal Aircraft Factory at Farnborough four years earlier. Building and then flying aeroplanes was a profession barely a dozen years old following the Wright brothers' fantastic invention in 1902.

G. Holt Thomas who had set up the Aircraft Manufacturing Company (usually known as Airco) wanted a designer and recruited de Havilland, who became chief designer. The firm was based at Grove Park (see p.78) and had its works on the Edgware Road. From the fields in front of Grove Park Mansion the test flight took place, in 1916, of the DH4 – their most famous wartime aircraft. All his designs bore the same initials through to the DH106, the famous Comet, the first British all-jet airliner, in 1949 and the DH121, the Trident, one of the world's favourite passenger airplanes.

The end of the First World War in 1918, led to an inevitable slump in the demand for military aircraft, while the demand for civilian aircraft had hardly begun. Airco was sold to BSA (Birmingham Small Arms) who were not in that business. Geoffrey de Havilland – with the others of Airco – was out of a job. A pilot, whom the people at Airco knew well, who had had a serious accident and lost a limb, married one of the staff – he went on, with his brother, to make artificial limbs at the that site – he was Marcel, one of the Desoutter brothers, whose factory was at the Edgware Road site until about ten years ago.

Generously, Holt Thomas helped de Havilland to set up on his own at nearby Stag Lane Aerodrome. What had brought this about in the first place was the proximity of Hendon Aerodrome, a major military aviation centre. With the rapid development of wartime uses for planes, Kingsbury and the Edgware Road became expansion areas for the main centre for the RAF (as it developed from the wartime Royal Flying Corps). W.T. Warner and M.G. Smiles who set up the London and Provincial Aircraft Company there opened Stag Lane as an aerodrome in 1916. Their main work was as a flying school, but with the end of the war, this work also ceased (as had Airco's). They then started making chocolates and, as Geoffrey de Havilland writes in his autobiography, 'of this they knew nothing but left a sticky mess which we had to clear up'. They were able to offer a lease to de Havilland in 1920, and the following year, sold it to him outright.

Over the years that followed, de Havilland expanded with new hangars, extended workshops, sawmills and erecting bays. Aircraft production soared and staff grew in numbers from 50 to 1,000. As an article years later remembered, power for heating in winter in the design office hut was provided by an old aero-engine, running on coal gas. In summer, they ate sandwiches under the nearby trees. Sir Alan Cobham operated taxi services from Stag Lane and a by-product of the de Havilland Company was a School of Flying and the London Aero Club, where Amy Johnson worked for a while as an engineer, after learning to fly.

The success of the company as a force to be reckoned with in the aviation world was confirmed with the production of the DH60 Moth in 1925. As Geoffrey de Havilland reported to his company's Annual General Meeting in 1926, 'not only is it the standard training machine for light aeroplane clubs, but enquiries are continuously being received from all parts of the world'. From it was developed the even more famous Tiger Moth, in 1931, which became the standard military training aircraft.

It was not only Amy Johnson who used Stag Lane, but also Jim Mollison, Jean Batten, Lady Bailey, the Duchess of Bedford, Billy Cotton, comedian Will Hay and many others better-known in aviation circles than to the wider world. Jean Batten said, 'it was not a good aerodrome for it sloped quite steeply [...] during the winter it became quite sodden in places and it was difficult to taxi through the mud'.

Amy Johnson created many flying records, some with Jim Mollison to whom she was married for about four years. She made the first solo flight by a woman across the Atlantic and she was the first woman to fly solo to Australia – a daring feat she undertook in May 1930. For this she was awarded the CBE. She was killed in the last war in 1941, when the aeroplane she was ferrying blew up over the Thames Estuary. On the aerodrome estate, there are road names: Mollison Way and de Havilland Road and Amy Johnson Court. Yet another member of staff, for a while, was a mathematician called N.S. Norway who turned to writing novels under his first names – Neville Shute.

What had been open fields in 1916 had seen not only the commercial development of the aerodrome, but also encroaching suburbia. With the creation of 'Queensbury' at the beginning of the 1930s, de Havilland realised they could sell the aerodrome site profitably and use the money to move to a larger site, at Hatfield. Stag Lane closed in 1934 (with only the Engine Division remaining, until 1969). A housing estate took over and, within two years, there were 1,000 houses built.

De Havillands continued to prosper at Hatfield, producing successful wartime aircraft such as the Mosquito and civil aeroplanes like the Trident. They later went through a series of mergers, ultimately becoming part of British Aerospace. Geoffrey met his American cousins,

Stag Lane Airfield in 1923. (Courtesy BAe)

Above: Engineers at work in the de Havilland aeroshop at
Stag Lane.

Right: Sir Geoffrey de Havilland.

Olivia de Havilland and Joan Fontaine the film stars, on a number of occasions both here and
in the USA. His three sons shared his work, though tragically two of them were killed, while
acting as test pilots. He was knighted in 1944 and received the Order of Merit in 1962. He died
in 1965. He was one of the giants of the aviation world and, to his staff at Stag Lane, a hero for
the work he created there.

Sudbury Town
Station, 1916.
(Courtesy
London's Transport
Museum, Transport
for London)

The Admirable Sudbury Town Station

I know we all get frustrated and even angry from time to time when the Tube service lets us down. Yet, we know in our hearts that London's Underground has been the envy of the world for well over a hundred years. After the very first, the Metropolitan Railway from Paddington to Farringdon via King's Cross, built by 'cut and cover' mainly under Euston Road, it was soon evident that it was to be the forerunner of a remarkable transport network.

The beginnings of the deep level modern Tube came with the City and South London in 1890, from Stockwell to near the Bank – now part of the Northern Line. I am not writing a history of the Tube here (there are plenty of excellent books on that absorbing topic) but it is worth recalling that in the first few years of the twentieth century, five Tube lines were constructed and they were soon brought together as the United Electric Railways of London (UERL).

One of these, the District Line, reached Ealing Broadway in West London way back in 1879; a new branch was built in 1903 to South Harrow through Park Royal (to serve the Royal Agricultural Show, Alperton (originally named Perivale-Alperton) and on to South Harrow. In 1910 it was extended to Uxbridge via Rayners Lane, sharing the line with the Metropolitan. An enormous viaduct took the line across the river Brent and into Alperton Station. Much of this extension ran through green fields and there is still a little of the old rural atmosphere if you stand on the hump-backed bridge in Allendale Road in Sudbury and look down the tracks. The line though this part of Middlesex was part of the deliberate and planned policy of the railway companies to encourage suburban communities to develop by providing the easy means of transport into the centre of the metropolis – the best example being 'Metroland'. Especially after the First World War, suburbia reached out to embrace those green fields and convert them to brick and tile.

By about 1908, the driving force behind the new UERL was the team of Albert Stanley (later Lord Ashfield) and Frank Pick who worked together for over thirty years to make the London Underground and then London Transport as a whole, the system we have come to know and respect. One of the first efforts at unifying the service was the very name of the railways for which the logo was created as 'UndergrounD'.

Sudbury Town
Station, 1934.
(Courtesy London's
Transport Museum,
Transport for
London)

Frank Pick was born in Lincolnshire in 1879 and worked all his life in the railway industry, coming to London in 1906 to join the new Tube service. As commercial manager of UERL, Frank Pick used his flair for the visual arts to great effect. He established consistent design framework covering lettering, vehicles, posters, station furniture and so on. He commissioned specially designed posters advertising the interesting and exciting places which could be reached by Tube (a display of these can be seen at the London Transport Museum in Covent Garden). He conceived a range of lettering consistently used throughout the network, uniquely devised by the renowned typographer Edward Johnstone – it is known as 'London's handwriting' and instantly recognisable. He employed artists like McKnight Kauffer and sculptors like Eric Gill and Epstein. He recognised the genius of the architect Charles Holden. Pick developed, from an earlier device, the famous roundel, internationally recognised, with the word 'Underground' or the station name on a blue bar across a red circle on a white background – you know it even before I have finished describing it.

With these elements of artistic design and the hand-picked artists to carry·out his vision, Pick created a strong corporate identity which became especially important and significant when the publicly-owned London Passenger Transport Board – the creation of Herbert Morrison the then Labour minister – was brought into existence in 1933. Ashfield became chairman and pick managing director – a brilliant team aptly suitable at the right time and the right place.

Pick was very keen on using Tube station design as the way to convey the sense of unity of purpose for the travelling public and this was where Holden came to his aid. In the 1920s he had designed many stations such as Bond Street on the Central Line and Tooting Bec on the Northern. Then, in the early 1930s, Sudbury Town became his original design for stations on the Uxbridge branch of the district before it was transferred to the Piccadilly Line in 1932. It is described in *The Moving Metropolis* (published for the London Transport Museum) as a brick-work design, echoing the neighbouring suburban houses (in Station Approach). Its walls support a reinforced concrete roof and the large windows provide light for the spacious booking hall. The globe lighting outside is one more example of the attention to detail in the whole design.

No wonder it was properly given listed building status, which protects its design from destruction or inappropriate alterations. Each platform is reached without any stairs, making it one of the few accessible stations for physically handicapped persons. How different from Alperton, the next station down the line, on its viaduct (though it did boast, for a few years, one of the escalators from the Festival of Britain), or from Sudbury Hill, both requiring a lot of stairs to be traversed, but otherwise exquisitely designed by Holden.

The building programme was extended along the Piccadilly Line to the north-east including Arnos Grove and Turnpike Lane. However, in the period after the Second World War, there was never quite the same consistency and tenacity of design on the Underground until we get to the Jubilee Line extension in the 1990s out to Stratford.

Ashfield and Pick ran the new LPTB with enviable success for about seven years until the Second World War. Pick died in 1941. Ashfield continued his life-long work in charge of the London Transport Executive which was set up within the British Transport Commission (which brought the whole of inland transport under one colossal publicly-owned management in 1947). Ashfield died the following year, aged seventy-four. 'The contribution of the experienced, far-sighted, politically acute chairman with the brilliant chief of staff provided a balance of flexibility in approach with rigorous management which made the London Transport Board an object of (sometimes unwilling) admiration,' wrote Barker and Robbins in *A History of London Transport*, (1974).

What was said about Sir Christopher Wren after rebuilding London and particularly St Paul's Cathedral could equally be applied to Ashfield and Pick: 'if you seek their monument – look around you'. The Tube is full of reminders of their genius.

It's a Mauve One – Perkin, the Discoverer of Aniline Dyes

Have you ever thought how the colour came to your shirt or blouse? We are so used to seeing an enormous variety of colours in these materials that we may not realise how much we owe to one man. Until the experiments by the young William Henry Perkin succeeded in creating the first synthetic dye, those that were used to colour fabrics had to be obtained from nature.

Plants, wood, minerals and animals (insects and molluscs) were pressed into service to obtain the dyes. The materials came from all over the world – indigo from Brazil, cochineal from Mexico, madder from the Near East, and so on. The problem was that these sources produced only a limited range of colours – mainly reds and blues; many were fugitive – that is they lost colour when exposed to sunlight, which is hardly the best recommendation for selling a shirt or an umbrella.

William Perkin was born in East London in 1838, the son of a builder. At school, he became fascinated by chemistry and was soon doing advanced work. He was able to carry out research projects and one of these, by chance (it often happens that way – think of the way Fleming 'found' penicillin), led him to the discovery of a dye from an aniline base, which was purple in colour – and stable!

As a result of his work, he was able to take out a patent in August 1856, when he was only eighteen years old (apparently, strictly speaking he was too young, but that was not a serious hindrance). His invention was described by him 'of a colouring matter for dyeing with a Lilac or Purple Colour, Stuffs of Silk, Cotton, Wool or other Materials'.

Armed with this patent and with the knowledge of his own skill, he made an incredible decision – he dropped further studies and decided to become an industrialist. With the backing of his father (who became a sort of sleeping partner) and his elder brother, Thomas, he set up a

Sir William Perkin.

factory at Greenford Green – near the Black Horse Inn on Oldfield Road (the modern firm of Glaxo Wellcome now own part of the site).

A.S. Travis wrote that:

> Perkin's genius lay not only in his persistence and patience in continued investigation of the unknown and apparently unsuccessful chemical reaction, but also in realising the commercial possibilities for what was, after all, only a minor product. The back room experiment was about to become the pot of gold at the end of a synthetic rainbow of dyes.

Actually, it was not quite so straightforward, as converting the laboratory experiment into a usable commercial product turned out to be quite complicated. Perkin worked with the leading dyer of the day, Pullar's of Perth, to overcome the technical problems. The Greenford factory began to produce what was called aniline (or Tyrian) purple. Perkin travelled widely in Europe to advise dyers how to use it. The French took it up and called it 'mauve' – the first time that name was used. Soon, it started appearing in novels and articles, as if it had been around for years. Perkin himself called it, in 1863, mauvine. His work was bringing him international fame.

In his personal life, he had more mixed fortunes. In 1859, he married his cousin Jemima Harriet Lisset and they moved into Seymour Villa on the Harrow Road, Sudbury, conveniently near Greenford Green. They had two sons, but, tragically, Jemima died of tuberculosis in 1862. Perkin was heartbroken.

Five years later, he married the daughter of a neighbour and they raised a further family, including two girls, Lucy and Sasha. The firm prospered, but success and foreign competition – and perhaps his family concerns, brought Perkin to the decision to sell the Greenford factory. Thus at the early age of thirty-six, he retired, wealthy enough to lead the life of a country squire. He built a house for himself next door to Seymour Villa, called 'The Chestnuts', using his old home as a research laboratory. He had stopped being an industrialist, but he could not forsake his original love for chemistry.

He joined in the work of the local community at Sudbury. He built the New Hall to replace a makeshift workman's hall and cottages; there was also a Sunday school. Although a Methodist, he helped other local churches with money. His old home was pulled down some years ago, but is recalled by the names like Chestnut Grove and there is Perkin Close. He was knighted in 1906 and died, full of honours, especially from his profession, in July 1907. His daughter, Sasha, became a missionary, but came home to Sudbury in 1939 to unveil a plaque at his centenary, in Butler's Green Sudbury. One of his sons, who bore the same name, William Henry, became a university professor at Manchester and inspired Chaim Weizmann, a renowned chemist himself, who helped the Allied war effort in 1914-18 and later became President of Israel. Thus, Perkin's influence spread far and wide from that first discovery while at school in London in 1856.

The Babington Plot

'Hush,' said Katherine Bellamy, 'Walsingham's spies may not be far off. We must take especial care'. These words were nearer the truth than she knew and her family's safety was almost overturned. At that moment, a scared, bedraggled fugitive had rushed into the house: Anthony Babington.

The background to this illuminating story is the struggle which Queen Elizabeth I had to protect her new Protestant English kingdom from the threats made by Catholics, led from inside prison since 1568, by her cousin Mary Queen of Scots. Elizabeth's Secretary of State, Walsingham organised the counter-campaign on his Queen's behalf, together with her principal adviser, Sir William Cecil (later Lord Burleigh). He laid down strict rules to try to prevent Catholics practicing their faith, with even stricter penalties if they disobeyed. Jesuit missions were sent from Europe to try to strengthen the true believers. Walsingham invented 'dirty tricks' to trap them.

In the 1580s, the Bellamys had been living at Uxendon Manor, on the western side of Barn Hill in Wembley, for many years. William had married into another well-known local family when he wed Katherine Page. They and their children lived comfortably, as farmers, and practicing their

Right: St Robert Southwell.

Opposite: Sasha Perkin and pupils at the New Hall Sunday School, Sudbury (near William Perkin's home) August 1899.

religion as quietly and safely as they could, but with one, ultimately fatal, secret: they offered refuge to fugitive Catholics, especially priests on their missions from their training college run by Dr William Allen at Douai College in Belgium and later in Reims in northern France. No refuge was more well-known to the conspiratorial circle than Uxendon. Among the leading Catholic Jesuit agents who used Uxendon and knew the Bellamys were Edmund Campion and Robert Persons (who was one of the few to escape execution for keeping to his faith).

The building no longer exists, but it needs only a little stretch of the imagination to fill it with false doors, priest holes, secret passages (out to a wooded part of Barn Hill) or the hidden chamber from which another subterranean passage led to a nearby barn.

Meanwhile, Walsingham's spies tracked the proud but hunted priests and many of them were caught in different hiding places in England and executed in the Tower. But there was also the problem of Mary Queen of Scots who, although imprisoned at Fotheringhay, was trying to spin a web to ensnare Elizabeth. Walsingham willingly stepped in to help by 'framing' a young, vain Catholic named Anthony Babington. He lent himself to the leadership of a conspiracy to put Mary on the throne, set out in a letter to Mary, which was probably drafted by Walsingham. One of Bellamy's Catholic friends was John Gerard, whose cousin was the Protestant Master of the Rolls, Sir Gilbert Gerard who, coincidentally, lived nearby Uxendon at Sudbury Hill.

It is August 1586. Babington and his co-conspirators are now on the run – part of the 'cat-and-mouse' tactics of the Secretary of State – and he and his co-plotters fled to St John's Wood (which was then what its name suggests) and from there to the 'safety' of Uxendon Manor. There Walsingham's men caught them, despite Katherine Bellamy's whispered warning quoted at the start of this story. They were summarily executed 'with a brutality that shocked even those onlookers begging for his blood' (Alice Hogge, *God's Secret Agents*).

This gave Walsingham the chance to persuade the very reluctant Queen Elizabeth to sign the death warrant for her cousin. Mary was executed on 8 February 1587. Philip of Spain was so shocked by this act that he prepared to attack England and the Armada set out on its fateful voyage the following year.

DON SHOOTING SCHOOL CLUB
NEAR HARROW
TELEPHONE Nº1 WEMBLEY
IGRAMS UXENDON WEMBLEY

Uxendon Manor in the early twentieth century when it was a shooting ground. (Courtesy Geoffrey Hewlett)

There was even worse to follow for the brave but foolhardy Bellamys, at whose house the dire arrest was made. Katherine was brought before Walsingham and probably tortured, though she died before she could be executed. Three of her four sons also died or were 'judicially' murdered as a result of their capture. Only Thomas was able to continue his life at Uxendon until he had to sell it in 1603.

Yet, there was more to come involving his daughter Anne and the priest Robert Southwell, who is commemorated in the name of a school at Kingsbury (as is another of the band of foolhardy but brave Catholics, Margaret Clitherow, who was canonised at the same time as Southwell in 1970). Anne's brother Thomas knew Southwell and so Anne was keen for him to visit Uxendon. However, this was part of a horrible plot. Anne had been arrested because of her faith and the thereby came into contact with the notorious Richard Topcliffe, a one-time MP who had become the chief persecutor of Catholics and described as a monster for his tortures. He raped her and then forced her into marriage with one of his associates, at the same time 'persuading' her to betray Southwell. On 25 June 1592, Topcliffe hastened to Uxendon and gleefully arrested his victim. Southwell's terrible death, as a martyr, in 1595 was the cause that lead to his canonisation.

Uxendon Farm remained under many different owners for many years, before ending its days as a shooting range. Then, ironically, this site, set in the heart of Metroland, fell victim to the Metropolitan Railway's extension to Stanmore (now the Jubilee Line) in the 1930s and no trace of it remains.

Park Royal – Caring and Cars

On the southern edge of Brent, spilling over into Ealing is the district known today as Park Royal. The name conjures up a magical mixture of the imperial and the rural. Yet of all the local names, this is one of the newest – barely one hundred years old. The story behind the name is fascinating, but begins one thousand years ago.

View of industry along the Grand Union Canal at Park Royal in the 1920s.

133/24   Grand Union Canal, Park Royal

In Domesday Book, prepared for William the Conqueror in 1087, our district is recorded under Willesden, Harlesden and both West and East Twyford. At that time they belonged to St Paul's Cathedral – a situation which remained until the Reformation – giving rise to street names such as Dean Road and Chapter Road. Over the centuries, they remained small isolated farming communities originally set up by Anglo-Saxon tribes seeking to create farms and homesteads for themselves.

West Twyford was transferred to Ealing in 1926; East Twyford had a small manor house called Lower Place and it also contained farms such as Ruckholts or Little Lower Place Farm. There was also a house marked on John Roque's famous 1746 map of London which was taken over and rebuilt by Thomas Willan in 1806, using the same architect who created Abbotsford for the author Sir Walter Scott. With its Gothic windows, battlements and fake medieval appearance it was an amazing but delightful building set down in this out-of-the-way part of Middlesex. Willan called it Twyford Abbey, although it was never intended for monastic purposes. By the strangest coincidence, a genuine monastic order, the Alexian Brothers, bought it in 1902 and they used it as a hospice until giving it up in 1998, since which time it has, sadly been empty and decaying.

In 1801, the Paddington branch of the Grand Junction Canal (later part of the Grand Union system) was built right through southern Willesden and in 1837 the London and Birmingham Railway (see p.25) came close to being a few hundred yards apart at Acton Lane. Between them, the railway and the canal changed the face of Britain for ever and underpinned the Industrial Revolution. The quiet fields of Twyford were not to remain bucolic for much longer.

Now, we leap forward to 1894 when the Medical Officer of Health for Willesden, who was charged with maintaining and recording the well-being of its citizens, reported that 'there had been improvements in the general health over the past year'. The birth rate was 30.7 per 1,000, compared with 28.8 in England and Wales, while the death rate of 12.25 compared well with the national 16.9. Only in infant deaths was the district faring not so well. These raw figures make a strong point. Willesden was doing quite well in looking after its people. A new cottage hospital had just been opened in Harlesden Road, thanks to the benefaction of the Cornishman, John Passmore Edwards.

Barrett's Green Nursery,
Park Royal, 1928.

Meanwhile, in that remote south west corner, something was happening which was intended to help the poorest in the parish. The poor laws had been developed in Elizabethan times to deal with vagrancy, unemployment and to give some limited help to the old and infirm. Poor Law Districts were set up in the charge of boards of guardians. Willesden was covered by the Hendon Union. However, in October 1895, one of the Willesden members, Frederick Priest, began a campaign to give his parish its own Poor Law District. One of the strong arguments he put forward was that, of the 350 inmates of the crowded Hendon workhouse, 250 were from Willesden alone. He won his case and within the year, Willesden had its own control over the poor law rules.

The Board of Guardians – and they were quite powerful in their part of what we would now call social services – elected as its chairman a Middlesex County Councillor, Mr J.A. Adams (he was also a Conservative Party agent, though the role of political agents was not and never has been a problem in local activity). The important post of clerk was taken over by the thirty-year old Mr J. Hutton Haylor who stayed in the post until his death in 1938, at the age of seventy-two.

The search for a site for the Willesden workhouse and infirmary, led the board to buy about sixty acres on the Ruckholt or Little Lower Place Farm from the family of Thomas Willan. They would later become one of the most valuable sixty-acre plots in Willesden. The architect, Mr A. Saxon Snell, designed the new institution, for which the foundation stone was laid in April 1900 by the board's chairman, with other local big-wigs present. Bands played, prayers were offered up; speeches were made.

It was planned as six double-ward blocks of two storeys for over 600 inmates and would have been the largest institution in Willesden – but all that the funds raised allowed to be built was enough to accommodate 150 sick people and 250 workhouse inmates, the sick and infirm. It opened in March 1903. The workhouse master (shades of Mr Bumble – though that is probably quite unfair to the new incumbent) and matron were Mr and Mrs Joseph Brierley and the matron of the hospital section was Miss M.H. Frost who had been at the Willesden Cottage Hospital in 1893. The buildings still form the central portion of Central Middlesex Hospital, although further redevelopment may signal the end of this historic edifice. The workhouse was sometimes known as Twyford Lodge, a euphemism to give a sense of respectability, especially to illegitimate children born there. Willesden parish also ran a 'Scattered Homes System' for children, from 1914 and had a nursery at the hospital and later a children's home in Barrett's Green Road.

Guinness at Park Royal – under construction, 1934.

Royal Agricultural Show at Park Royal – the entrance in 1903.

What happened was that the new infirmary and workhouse continued to function in a dual role, until, gradually, its hospital role took over more and more. At the same time, the national mood was turning away from the restrictive attitudes engendered by the poor laws which were so vividly described by Charles Dickens in many of his novels. Lloyd George introduced National Insurance in 1911. Other measures towards what would become the welfare state were passed by Parliament until the Local Government Act of 1929. This transferred the poor law functions to the local council and Willesden now became responsible for the infirmary. The name was soon changed to Central Middlesex Hospital (although it was also called the Park Royal Hospital, from its obvious location). Nearly half of the land to the north became Willesden Council allotments.

The introduction of the National Health Service in 1948 brought the Central Middlesex into the fold of the ubiquitous caring provision, though the subsequent fluctuations in organisation, usually politically inspired, have done little to impair its reputation for looking after the people of Willesden at times when illness overtook them. Its history suggests it will long continue to be welcomed in this role.

Meanwhile, in 1904, the Royal Agricultural Society opened its show just to the west of the workhouse and, as it was opened by the Prince of Wales, it was named Park Royal. After the show closed it had a number of uses. Queen's Park Rangers made it one of their many early grounds. It became a depot for the Dairy Milk Supply Company (part of the Express Dairy) and then was taken for military purposes during the First World War.

When the war was over, in the mid-1920s, industry geared up and many small engineering firms moved in – buildings were erected on new industrial estates. It became especially attractive to motor car manufacturers and the road names still remind us of that era – Standard, Sunbeam and Minerva. Soon the hospital was almost surrounded by industrial buildings, with the exception of the land to the north which became allotments. In 1934, Guinness moved in to create their large London brewing plant.

More was to come. In the 1980s, Brent and Ealing Councils came together to promote the regeneration of the now rather run-down Park Royal estate. The author was on the committee which set the pace for what has become the largest industrial redevelopment in Western Europe and as a result, an immense change has swept over the whole area, even absorbing the allotments and enabling Central Middlesex Hospital to be rebuilt.

Who could have guessed from the Domesday Book what today's 'Twyford' would be like and how valuable this land of five villagers and one hundred and fifty pigs worth sixty shillings would have become in 1900.

The Empire comes to Wembley

About fifty years after the Great Exhibition, which produced the Crystal Palace in Hyde Park, the idea was born of a great display to celebrate the British Empire – then at its zenith after Queen Victoria's death. It took another twenty years – a delay partly caused by the First World War – before the dream became a reality. The vision of Lord Strathcona was taken up by Lord Stevenson, with the then Prince of Wales (later Edward VIII) as the president of the general committee offering royal support right from the start. A general manager was appointed, V.F. Wintour. He and others involved are remembered in street names on a nearby housing estate.

The first Cup Final at Wembley, 1923.

Aerial view of the British Empire Exhibition, Wembley, 1924.

The first problem was to find a site, and it soon became clear that the now derelict Wembley Park Amusement Ground was the best in London – although Wembley Council had tried to buy a part of it for housing, which would have ruined the plans. The Prince of Wales recognised the value of sport in the set-up of such a display of the Empire's scope and thus the idea of the Wembley Stadium was born.

Work started in 1922, with the intention that the British Empire Exhibition (as it had come to be called) would open the following year. However, it became clear that more time was needed – thus the stadium was open a year ahead of the main events. The park is set in a small dip (where the Wealdstone brook runs through on its way to join the Brent) and on the southern hill where the remains of 'Watkin's Folly' were recalled by four large craters. The stadium bowl was excavated and the concrete for the stands (to a design by Owen Williams) was poured in, section by section – including the world-famous Twin Towers which became an international symbol of football, but were demolished with the rest of the original building to allow the new stadium to be created.

Although it is another great story, it is worth recalling that the first Cup Final to be played here was between West Ham and Bolton (Bolton won 2–0) and the PC on the white horse, Constable George Scorey, will always be remembered for the way he restored order among the crowd of 200,000.

Meanwhile, the local council, the Metropolitan Railway and the bus companies had been working to improve the ways to get masses of people to the new stadium and exhibition. Roads were widened, including Forty Lane and Empire Way (renamed in honour of the great event); Wembley Park Station was rebuilt and a bus station was created on the edge of the grounds (this was said to be the first of its kind in the world).

Above: Girls from Brondesbury and Kilburn High School visiting the British Empire Exhibition in 1924.

Right: Sir Arthur Elvin who saved Wembley Stadium from oblivion.

Opposite: The amusement park at the British Empire Exhibition, 1924.

The main exhibition buildings – at the whole cost about £30 million (in contemporary terms) – were made of the same grey Ferro-concrete as the stadium, while many of the colonial stands were brightly coloured replicas of their countries' architecture.

On St George's Day 1924 (appropriately), King George V opened the exhibition, his words, for the first time, being broadcast by the new BBC. Mention must be made of the Never-Stop Railway. Because the site was so large, a way had to be found to make it easier for visitors to get round it. The railway was built as a loop line running at a pace that gave 'passengers ample time to sit and see without the labour of walking'. You got on and off while it was still moving at an even slower pace; it went from the south to the north end and back again – hence, North End Road.

One of the cigarette kiosks (later he expanded it to eight) was run by a young ex-serviceman and ex-POW, Mr A.J. Elvin. As the exhibition (which had been so successful that it was reopened in 1925) came to its close, he saw an opportunity to use the unwanted buildings as scrap. Some buildings were transferred in their entirety – the Palestine building became a Glasgow laundry! Elvin then seized an opportunity to buy the stadium, raised the money and ran it for many years, steering it to even greater successes. He was knighted and became a Freeman of Wembley. Under his control, Wembley expanded its activities to become the 'Sports Centre of the Empire'. There was greyhound racing ('the dogs'), speedway racing, six-day cycle races and with the opening in 1934 of the Empire Pool (which, sadly, closed when the war came and never regained its earlier role) took on swimming in summer and ice-skating in winter. The greatest event of all was the Olympic Games held here in 1948 with the marathon ending, spectacularly, in front of the Royal Box. Sir Arthur Elvin died in 1957, known as the man who created the Wembley that is now about to end.

Wembley Stadium, seen across the lake at the British Empire Exhibition in 1924.

Carrying the Olympic torch on the last lap into the Olympic Stadium at Wembley, 1948 (one of the torches is in the Mayor's parlour at Brent Town Hall).

Elsewhere on the exhibition site, the story is less attractive. The area surrounding the stadium was developed piecemeal as a trading estate and it took, for example, many years for the company who owned it and the borough council to agree on completing the roads which crossed the site (First Way, Second Way and so on). Now it looks set for a massive redevelopment, in the wake of the rebuilding of the stadium itself. Thus the wheel comes full circle.

six

A Brent Miscellany

The Ladysmith Road Murder

The last thing on George Crossman's mind that day in March 1904 was the local council elections in Willesden. What did occupy his mind – and he boasted about it – was the body of the woman in the trunk in the attic in that house in Ladysmith Road in Kensal Rise.

George Albert Crossman was a small, rather sallow-faced man, in his thirties; he had a dark, drooping moustache and soft dark eyes. He had grown up where he was born in Kilburn in 1872, but life had treated him badly – or was it the other way round? He was a gambler and a thief – he served at least two short terms in jail in 1891 and 1892. He could not hold down a job, he used different names to cover his tracks and, according to his relatives he was – the worst accusation of all – an atheist!

He found his real profession in … bigamy. His first wife, who gave him a child (according to his own statement), died in 1897 – possibly murdered by Crossman, though this was never brought to light. By the time she died, he was already courting his next victim, Miss Ethel Anne Farley. He married her in Maidstone in May 1897 and took his bride to live in Ilford. They seemed to live a reasonably harmonious married life – or so Ethel thought. He was arrested the following year, for passing a bogus cheque. Ethel only learnt of this on a visit to her parents in Maidstone. Worse than this, she was horrified to discover that, while she was away on that visit to her parents in Kent, her beloved George had persuaded a young West End housemaid, Mary Ann Osborne (we are beginning to see that Crossman seems to have had a fancy for the name Ann) to marry him. This took place, with all the audacity in the world, in All Saints' church on 16 November 1898. What was in his mind as the words of the marriage service 'do you know of any impediment …' were uttered?

Ethel and Mary met at the Old Bailey in December; their eyes exchanged sad glances as their 'husband', no longer charged for merely passing a dud cheque but with bigamy, stood trial. It was an open and shut case and Crossman was sentenced to five years' hard labour (as it was then described).

Then, in 1902, 'this infamous scoundrel' as *The Willesden Chronicle* was to describe him, was released on 'ticket-of-leave' (an early form of parole) to continue his Bluebeard career. He was now living at Ladysmith Road with another 'wife', Miss Edith Thompson, telling her that he was working as a newspaper reporter to cover up his frequent absences. He had met her in response to an advertisement she had placed in a newspaper for a lady's help. Then in January 1903, calling himself Mr Seymour, he got married again at the West London Registry office to a nurse, Ellen Sampson, a widow - telling his resident wife (Edith) in Ladysmith Road that he was going away to Manchester to do a special report for his newspaper and sent her home to her parents in Worcester Park in South London. He took his latest wife to Ladysmith Road and there killed her on 16 January – a tragically short married life for poor Ellen.

Wrentham Avenue, called Ladysmith Road when built – home of the gruesome murderer George Albert Crossman, after his trial the name was changed.

He found it possible, in August 1903, under another alias, this time Mr Weston, an 'architect', to marry a Miss Venables at Richmond parish church, pleading business as a baker on night duty to explain his frequent absences, but praying diligently at home in Richmond and regularly visiting the church on Sunday, thus belying his supposed atheism, or building another layer of lies to support his latest venture into matrimony. He was alternating, Box and Cox fashion between there and Ladysmith Road, spending three or four days at each home.

In January 1904, he went on to 'marry' Miss Annie Welch, at St George's church in Reading (he had met her in November, telling her he was Frank Seaton, when she was a maid in service at Rutland Gate in London, so that going way out of town for the wedding was a careful protection for him). They went for a week to 43 Ladysmith Road and found it already tenanted by another wife (Edith) who, George told Annie, was his cousin and housekeeper and who had a baby which he said was that of his dead wife. He then took Annie to Whitstable and then to Herne Bay, but his behaviour (as 'Seaton') upset her, especially arousing her suspicions of another woman. Crossman forged her signature on her Post Office Savings Book and drew out her savings.

He had since brought Edith back home and during the next few weeks bought a tin box and a lot of cement, telling Edith that he was making a garden step. He was, indeed trying to dispose of Ellen's body. Meanwhile the lodgers downstairs, the Delfs, were becoming more and more worried about the terrible smell in the house, which Crossman told them was the drains. He sprayed the area with eau de cologne to try to cover up the odour.

On 23 March, the Delfs found a trunk which seemed to be the source of the terrible odour; George Crossman said he would arrange for it to be taken away but the van man, when he saw the box, refused. By this time Mr Delf had alerted the police and a constable came along to challenge Crossman. George then, thoroughly agitated, ran off along Dundonald Road then into Okehampton Road and into Hanover Road. Suddenly he put his hand to his throat and before PC Reeves could stop him, used his knife to fatal effect.

The coroner's inquest was reported in gruesome detail in *The Willesden Chronicle* of Friday 1 April 1904 – no April fool here. The body of Ellen Sampson, murdered on 16 January 1903 was released for burial more than a year after the tragedy; Crossman was buried in the unconsecrated part of Willesden Cemetery and peace returned to Ladysmith Road except that the residents, worried about the association of that name with the trunk murder, petitioned to the council for it to be changed. So, when you walk down Wrentham Avenue, you may be forgiven for not getting the shudders – you did not know it was once called Ladysmith Road...

Superloo Opens with Hullabaloo

The headline from *The Willesden Chronicle* of 6 April 1973 sums it up neatly and this is the story behind it.

Brent Council, in one of its expansionist phases had recognised the need for a public convenience on the Ealing Road. Soon after the Labour Party was returned to office in 1971, it had put money into its budget for this and the Chair of the Amenities and Works Committee, Ald Bob Thompson, set matters in motion.

A scheme was planned, architects were instructed and builders contracted to do the work. The new block was to cost £12,000 and would be the first to be built in Brent since it came into being in 1965. It was also the first to be purpose-built to provide for people with disabilities. It was tiled and provided not only hot and cold water but soap and towels too. Soon the toilets would be finished. What could be simpler?

This was the time when it was proudly announced that the first West Indian magistrates in Brent had been appointed – Mr Phil Sealy and Mr Vincent Crompton. And, on a more sinister note, the newspaper recorded that the National Front welcomed a visit by Mr Enoch Powell MP, though it was probably to that MP's dismay.

However, in Alperton, a tame, mundane piece of bureaucracy was about to spring into glorious Technicolor. It took its cue from the successful farce the BBC had presented, written by Ray Galton and Alan Simpson (who had already created *Steptoe* and *Hancock's Half Hour*). They had based it on the French folk comedy by Gabriel Chevalier which concerned the riotous happenings when the village of Clochemerle decided to build a men's convenience...

The opening of the new 'superloo' on the Ealing Road was not going to be as uproarious nor as upsetting as its fictional inspiration, but it would be an opportunity to show the world (the cliché became truer than expected) that Brent was in the forefront of civic pride.

It was prompted, I believe, by the then Public Relations Officer, Hilary Wilkinson and the Mayor, Cllr Bert Crane, and Alderman Bob Thompson responded with enthusiasm to the idea of a high-level rag as civic ceremony. Alperton High School and its head, Mr Roy Innes, joined in and provided a brass and wind band and a group of Sixth Form drama students.

The Mayor arrived together with a cloth-capped Freddie Earle, who was one of the stars of the TV series of *Clochemerle*. They were met by Ald Thompson who had walked from the school, with a group of students and then escorted to a dais in front of the then youth centre. A Union Jack and a French tricolour were draped across the building and acted as a backcloth to the ceremony. On the platform were also the late Roy Innes, Mrs Pauline Jackson of the Brent Association for the Disabled and the author's wife, Joan (the author was Chair of the Education Committee, but could not get away from work for the day – pity!).

The Mayor exchanged greetings with his fictional counterpart from *Clochemerle*, played by Freddie Earle. The band then opened with a fanfare 'Hail to the Toilet' and also played the finale, 'Toodle Loo', while the drama was written by Mr George Donnelly, a drama teacher at the school. The whole ceremony went off extremely well. The Mayor cut the tape formally to open the toilets and a few jokes with double meanings were heard from various dignitaries.

There were, it has to be recorded for historical accuracy, some dissenting voices, just as there were in the *Clochemerle* story. The local Baptist church, which was directly opposite, strongly objected to the 'degrading' type of ceremony and the vicar of nearby St James church also expressed his concerns. Even the leader of Brent Council, Ald Philip Hartley felt obliged to say: 'perhaps it is a bad thing to involve children in such a ceremony. But the opening of the toilets is a matter for general rejoicing'. This was the time of the Festival of Light, led by the late but respected Mary Whitehouse. Anything that smacked of a bit of impropriety came under scrutiny – even something as harmless as this. A Labour activist wrote to the paper (one of several letters from the public) complaining of the waste of ratepayers' money.

Away in Russia (and I thank the Old Alpertonians' newsletter for this snippet), *The New Times* wrote:

> A solemn ceremony in the small [sic] town of Brent near London was conducted by the Mayor himself. A new public building was being opened – the municipal toilet. All the local notabilities were present. Speeches were made. This way of glorifying their town was laid on by the authorities after watching the French comedy film *Scandal in Clochemerle* shown recently on British television.

They certainly had a good local stringer in Wembley!

Of course, as so often has happened in our local history, the building is no longer there. It was on the land of the old, original Alperton School which was sold to become a site for a new Hindu temple, now bravely being constructed. Its opening ceremony (when it takes place) will, I am sure, be just as colourful, but much more appropriate to the new occasion.

The Neasden Poisoner

I know they never taught poisons in the chemistry curriculum at John Kelly Boys' School. No blame can possibly be attached to the excellent teachers there to account for Graham Young's

Right: Graham Young, the Neasden Poisoner. (Courtesy Topham Picturepoint)

Opposite: Mayor Bert Crane and comedian Freddie Earle opening the Superloo in Ealing Road, Alperton, 6 April 1973. The toilets have long since been demolished.

growing obsession with chemistry and particularly the effects of poisons on the body. He was not quite fourteen when he dosed his sister Winifred with belladonna. When she fell sick, he apologised for his so-called mistake.

The man, who has been called 'the greatest British poisoner of the twentieth century', was born in Neasden on 7 September 1947. Sadly – and perhaps this loss is what later turned the young man towards dark pursuits – his mother died soon after he was born. He was brought up by an uncle and aunt for a couple of years until his father (who was a machine setter) remarried in 1950.

At Braintcroft Primary School, there was no sign of his later infamous behaviour – none that a later head teacher was aware of. His sister recalled nothing special about him, except that it seemed to her that he liked to be alone.

In his early teens, he became a fervent admirer of the Nazi movement and particularly of Hitler. He seems to have envied the dictator because of the power he wielded and wanted to emulate him. His use of poisons was to be the means by which he would obtain power over others.

He spent his pocket money buying small quantities of antimony and digitalis and later took to using thallium, another deadly poison. He claimed he needed these for experiments at school; he bought – so it was estimated – enough to kill three hundred people. Ugh! He put the poison into food for the family. His father, as well as his sister, fell sick and so did a friend. He himself – deliberately or not, it is not clear – suffered vomiting and cramps. His stepmother, Molly, died at Easter 1963 from his fatal dosages.

He was very quickly identified as the culprit and arrested. At his trial he was found insane and sent to Broadmoor. His sentence was for fifteen years, but by 1971 he was held to be no further threat to society and released. How wrong can you get?

Young obtained a job at a photographic instrument maker named John Hadland Ltd in Bovingdon, Hertfordshire. Within a few weeks of his arrival one man had died and seventy others had caught the 'Bovingdon bug'. It was not until October 1971, when another workman died, after suffering agonising back and stomach pains that it was realised that something was seriously amiss.

The police having been alerted, discovered that the poison thallium was the cause. They realised Young's previous Old Alpertonians' newsletter history (which no one had been aware of before at the factory) and arrested him. In 1972, he was tried at St Albans Crown Court on two charges of murder and four of attempted murder which he made no attempt to hide, at least in the words of the devastating diary he kept. He claimed that the notes on the victims were 'merely the basis for a novel'. He was probably still as unbalanced as when he had been sent to Broadmoor, but the jury this time handed in a verdict of guilty and he was sentenced to life imprisonment.

Our sympathies go out to his family who earlier survived his wicked plot and the relatives of those two workmen he remorselessly murdered, as well as the seventy who survived. Young himself died of a heart attack in Parkhurst Prison on 1 August 1990, a few weeks short of his forty-third birthday. What regrets did he take to a prison grave?

Mary Seacole – A Nurse to Remember

In Black History Month in October each year, one name will always come forward, in this part of London, to remind us that the black presence in Britain is not something that began with the arrival of the *Empire Windrush* in 1948. Soldiers from Africa served in the Roman army on Hadrian's Wall nearly two thousand years ago. From that date, as more research reveals, there has been an almost continuous inflow of settlers who are now seen as part of the background to our multi-cultural diversity.

Right: Mary Seacole wearing her Crimean War medals with pride. (Courtesy Helen Rappaport, National Portrait Gallery)

Opposite: Neasden Lane, as Young would have seen it in 1959.

Mary Seacole was born in Kingston, Jamaica, in 1805. Her father was a Scottish army officer named Grant and her mother a Jamaican healer, a 'doctress', who ran a boarding house for invalid officers. Mary grew up in a loving household and obtained a good education. She picked up some knowledge of medicine from her mother and became a skilled nurse. She was thirty when, in 1836, she married Edward Horatio Seacole, a godson of Lord Nelson. Tragically, her husband died not many months after the wedding. Worse was to come as her mother also died soon after that, leaving Mary on her own (it is not known when her father died).

Left to fend for herself, she succeeded by following in her mother's footsteps as a healer. With her family background, she was able to offer help to British soldiers stationed in Kingston and gained quite a lot of medical knowledge from some of the army doctors who were among her patients.

Soon she came to the realisation that she could do more with her life. She went off on several journeys round the Caribbean – where she and her late husband had spent a joyous few months before his sad demise. From there she went to America, along the southern states. This was a generation before the Civil War, where anti-black prejudice was already quite entrenched. However, she used her doctoring skills which helped pay her way. Having a good business sense, she set up stores across southern America, and even had a go at gold prospecting. She was a childless widow, with plenty of energy – what a woman!

She went to Panama (long before the canal was constructed) where there was a considerable amount of overland traffic transporting goods from the Caribbean to the west coast to save the long and treacherous journey round Cape Horn. She set up a hotel and then found many opportunities to use her nursing skills in a most dangerous part of the world. These experiences made her ready for the time ahead.

Mary Seacole's gravestone in St Mary's Cemetery at Kensal Green.

When Mary heard about the Crimean War, in 1854, she felt she had something to offer. She knew that the nursing system that served the British army was in a poor state – which was what had also appalled Florence Nightingale. She hurried to England to offer her services and went to the War Office, as it then was. To her surprise and dismay, she came up against race prejudice, which – perhaps naively – she had not expected to find in England. She spent months going unsuccessfully from one department to another. She tried to get an interview with the obvious person, Florence Nightingale, and also with Elizabeth Herbert, the wife of the War Minister, but both were denied. Although disheartened by these setbacks, she decided to travel to the Crimea, funding the venture from her own resources.

On arriving in Balaclava, she found that conditions for the wounded from the battlefields were as primitive and dilapidated as she had feared, despite some of the reforms Florence Nightingale had fought to secure. It is interesting that at least one reputable biographer of Miss Nightingale makes no reference to Mary Seacole.

Sickness was defeating the British army more than the Russians. So, Seacole used what money she had to set up medical stores and a hospice, the British Hotel. She often went to the front lines with medicines and food, becoming known as Mother Seacole. A soldier (quoted by Blacknet) said:

She was a wonderful woman [...] all the men swore by her, and in case of any malady, would seek her advice and use her herbal medicines [...] Her never failing presence amongst the wounded after a battle and assisting them made her beloved by the rank and file of the whole army.

In no time, her generosity of spirit was overcome by the fact that her money had run out. The sales of medicines, however well appreciated, could no longer sustain her efforts. She came back to London, as the war ended, destitute and in poor health. Her reputation came to her rescue. She wrote newspaper articles about experiences and then wrote her life story in a book, *The Wonderful Adventures of Mrs Mary Seacole in Many Lands*. Its success brought her popularity in Victorian England – and an income. She spent the rest of her life travelling between London and Kingston. Before she died in May 1881 she received many honours including the French Légion d'honneur. She was buried in St Mary's RC Cemetery at Kensal Green, where her gravestone reads, 'here lies a notable nurse who cared for the sick and wounded in the West Indies, in Panama and on the battlefield of the Crimea'.

Then she was forgotten for a hundred years until her reputation was retrieved in Brent. Then, a few years ago, her story was again told to the world and her brave exploits are now widely recognised – including the Florence Nightingale Museum – she was even listed as the greatest black British figure in history.

I finish with a quote from the recent Caribbean website 'The Dainty Crew':

This outstanding black woman devoted her life to caring, healing and tending to the sick and wounded at war. She overcame racial boundaries [...] she proved she was a fighter. Mary Seacole is a shining example to nurses of all races worldwide.

Trade Names

I would like to ask any reader of my generation to see if you have in your possession a Royal Sovereign pencil or a tin (or bottle) of Meltonian shoe polish, or perhaps a Smith's Sectric clock. What these all have in common is that they were all being made in Willesden fifty or so years ago.

The heyday of Willesden as a manufacturing area was the period roughly from 1910 to 1960, when a slow but unstoppable decline began, which has only recently been stemmed. There were – as there still are today – many small manufacturers as well as some large, nationally-known companies. I am concentrating here on the domestic side, leaving engineering firms for another time.

I wrote the draft of this with a ball-point pen. If I had been doing this some years ago it might well have been written in pencil and very likely a Royal Sovereign – just like the poet Philip Larkin who said that he wrote a series of his poems between 1955 and 1963 'with a succession of Royal Sovereign 2B pencils' – although I am not claiming to be in his class of writing at all!

The company was started in 1920 from an amalgamation of two older firms and settled in a factory in Neasden Lane to become one of the largest and best-equipped makers of their product in the world. At their peak they turned out three and a half million pencils a month. Even today you can buy, on the web, shop display cases of their pencils as souvenirs.

The 'lead' in their pencils was actually graphite mixed with varying amounts of clay which created the degree of hardness. The girls who made them would test them with circles and

Smith's Crisps delivery van, 1917.

squiggles on pieces of paper. The wood was cedar – you could get an exotic whiff of the scent each time you sharpened the pencil – the shavings taking with them a tiny fragment of the gold (or aluminium) paint used to stamp the name on the side of the pencils.

The regrettably short-lived *Willesden History Monthly* was only published in the year 1937; it carried many articles about life and activities in the borough and in March it had one headed 'Romance in Boot Polish'. This improbable headline referred to the Meltonian factory on the North Circular Road at Neasden. It had been built in the 1920s where the once-green fields overlooked the Welsh Harp – until the building of the new trunk road had attracted industry on the much-abused ribbon-building development.

The company had been started by a Mr Brown in Leicester Square in 1810 to make liquid blacking which was sold in stone jars. (Charles Dickens worked in a similar factory as a young lad). The name came from members of a hunting pack in the Leicestershire area of Melton Mowbray who were known in London as Meltonians. They were said to be the acme of smartness and this may well have had to do with their shiny hunting boots, polished with blacking. The Meltonian Company extended its products to include shoe polish and, over the years, became especially popular in the United States, which it still is, judging by the websites. It was also discovered to be useful as a dye for faded book cloth and was said to have 'a devout following among booksellers and an equally if more clandestine following among book repairers'. When the decline in manufacturing hit Willesden the firm was taken over by Reckitt & Colman and in turn their shoe care business was acquired by the Sara Lee Corporation in 1991. The Meltonian imp was used as their advertising device, and though it may long have disappeared, the polish it proclaimed lives on.

Smith's Sectric works, Temple Road.

Meltonian shoe works, Oxgate Lane, Dollis Hill, illuminated for the Silver Jubilee of King George V and Queen Mary.

Staples Mattresses – the name still applies to this junction where the North Circular Road crosses the Edgware Road. Although the original firm and building have long gone, a new company craftily using the same name enables the name to continue legitimately!

Eating healthy food is now a large-scale business and is the subject of wide-spread discussion on which diet to follow or which foods are good – or bad – for you. Back in Willesden seventy years ago, Mr R. Maurice started a firm to make healthy kinds of foods and was one of the first in this country to pick up a trend that was very popular on the Continent. This was Energen Foods whose best-known product was starch-reduced bread. Energen rolls are even today regarded by the Inland Revenue as bread to allow it zero-rating on VAT and Energen bran crisp is recommended to diet-conscious eaters for its fibre-richness.

The company started in a small way in Roundwood Road and then moved to newer premises in Bridge Road before coming to Cobbold Road in Willesden. In an interview in 1937 (in the *Willesden Illustrated Monthly* again) the Production Manager, Mr K.C. Wilson said that 'nowadays people have become more dietetically minded …They do not walk so much as they did; they have facilities for riding and so they ride instead of walking … Quite a lot of complaints that are prevalent at the present time are ascribable to an unsuitably balanced diet – an excess of starch'. Ah, well, 'plus ça change, plus c'est la même chose,' as they say.

The name of Smith is well known in Willesden industrial history – Smith's electrics and Smith's crisps being the most famous. This section is about Frank Smith who, about one hundred years ago, was manager of a wholesale grocery firm in the City of London. The proprietor brought across from France a recipe for thinly sliced potatoes cooked in oil. It took Frank's genius was to turn this simple idea into a world-beater. (The potato crisp had apparently been invented by an American chef named George Crum, in 1853, based on a similar French recipe, but he did not follow it up).

Starting up in Cricklewood, he soon expanded and then added his best idea – putting a small bag of salt in a blue twist of paper ('don't eat the blue crisp, Jack' as the joke went). The company continued to expand and to improve its cooking methods. Competition became fierce – Walkers being one of many to see opportunities in the field of snack foods. Then, as is almost inevitable in commerce today, its success led to its acquisition, in 1968, by the giant General Mills Company of America – and Smith's crisps – where are you now?

A little of what you fancy … especially if it is made locally. Even if some of the older firms have either gone completely or moved elsewhere, there are many new companies in the food business who find Brent a good place in which to produce that exciting something for your delectation.

Sporting Heroes

Brent has its fair share of sports personalities who have brought great renown to their chosen activities and fame to the district in which they were born or chose to make their home. Among a wide choice there are, for example Linford Christie, who lived in Harlesden; Luther Blissett the Watford and England football star and went to Willesden County Grammar School; Mike Gatting who went to John Kelly Boys' High School and, of course, more recently Audley Harrison of Kingsbury. I am concentrating on three special sporting heroes: Judy Grinham, Henry Cooper and Denis Compton.

Schools are often criticised today for failing to promote sport vigorously enough. However true or unfair this may be today, many of our sporting heroes received their first taste of their chosen sport at school or at a local centre run by the council such as Kingsbury Pool or Willesden or Vale Farm Centres.

Judy Grinham was brought up in Neasden and went to the Convent of Jesus and Mary. At the age of eighteen she became the first English swimmer to hold Olympic, European and Commonwealth (then known as Empire) titles at the same time.

She was born in 1939 and her family lived near Gladstone Park, whose outdoor pool gave her an early taste of the fluid joys of swimming. Her parents, as she acknowledges, were marvellous – prodding her in just the right direction and making sacrifices to assist her swimming career, since there was no help in those days for aspiring international athletes. Her father would meet her at Neasden station after training at Hampstead Ladies' Swimming Club which she joined when she was eleven. With all that happened in the next nine years, she later described this time as the period in her life when 'I was lucky enough to achieve all my hopes'. She quit soon after her twentieth birthday.

Her outstanding achievement, as the Willesden Borough Council proudly recorded in a certificate presented to her in December 1956, was to win the ladies' 100-metre back-stroke swimming event at the Melbourne Olympic Games of that year, creating a new Olympic record at that time of 1 minute, 12.9 seconds.

In May 1960 she wrote her autobiography, *Water Babe*, married the one-time sports editor of the local newspaper, *The Willesden Chronicle*, and retired from competitive sports – apparently she never swam again except for a little bit on holiday. She went on to bring up two children, in Northwood and has worked for many years for the Barnardo Association.

My next sporting hero is the one-time Wembley resident and greengrocer, Sir Henry Cooper – the greatest English heavyweight boxer of recent times. He was born in South London in May 1934. His family later moved to Ledway Drive, off Preston Road and his father ran a greengrocer's shop at the top of the Ealing Road. Many local people still recall being served by him, when he was a young man starting on his rise to boxing fame, with their potatoes and cauliflowers!

Judy Grinham.

He began his career in the ring in 1954 and in the course of seventeen years of fighting, gained the British, Commonwealth and European Heavyweight titles, including winning three Lonsdale belts outright although he never won the World title. He so nearly succeeded in his fight against Cassius Clay (later called Muhammad Ali). The knock-out punch he delivered came seconds before the end of the fourth round and Clay was 'saved by the bell'. Our 'Enry said 'we nearly had him - he was in trouble'. He retired in 1971 after just losing to Joe Bugner who was sixteen years younger. He is still around doing good work and looking well.

Denis Compton, OBE was born in Hendon on 23 May 1918 and went to Bell Lane School with his elder brother, Leslie. As a young lad he joined the ground staff at Middlesex Cricket Club at Lord's and by the time he was eighteen had won his first county cap and in 1938 made his debut for England against Australia. Later, after the war, he and his wife moved to Wembley – Retreat Close and Bowcroft Avenue.

One of the most fascinating aspects of Compton's life to most of us is the fact that he was a star at both cricket and football – he won a Cup Winners' medal playing for Arsenal in 1950 and then bowed out of first-class football. In fact he played a cricket match at the Highbury Stadium that year – it was his benefit match. He had already, in 1948, chalked up a remarkable cricket record of 3,816 runs and 18 centuries in that season. The Mayor of Wembley, full of civic pride, sent a telegram to Compton congratulating him on his magnificent innings of 145 not out at Old Trafford – which he completed after being hit in the face by a fast ball. In 1953, his innings helped win the Ashes again.

Right: (Sir) Henry Cooper.
(Courtesy National Portrait
Gallery)

Below: The Author and (Sir) Henry
Cooper.

Dennis Compton OBE hitting out! (Courtesy Topham Picturepoint)

His advertisements for Brylcreme created his image, accentuating the bronzed face and handsome physique which made him the most popular of all sporting stars in that post-war period of other great cricketers, not forgetting the Australian master, Don Bradman. He wrote a number of books including some autobiographical work such as *End of an Innings*. He was convivial, liking a drink with his fellow players. He loved South Africa, too – his second wife was from that country – though it would have been the country that had not yet liberated itself from the apartheid regime. He could still be described, not long after his death on St George's Day, 23 April 1997, by the writer Jeffrey Hill as 'one of the very small number of sportspeople who can be described as a "household name"'. That is how we surely remember him.

Baron of Wembley

During my time as chairman of one committee or another, my indispensable guide to the rules which help to make sensible debate work well was a little masterpiece called *The ABC of Chairmanship* by a writer called Walter Citrine. I came to learn that he had been one of the most influential men in Britain at one time. He became the longest serving general secretary of the Trades Unions Congress and was made Baron Citrine of Wembley.

Walter McLennan Citrine was born in 1887 in Wallasey and after leaving school at the age of twelve became an apprentice electrician. His experiences at work led him into the trade union movement and he joined the then Electrical Trades Union. He soon began his rapid rise to the top. In 1913 he married Doris Slade and they had two boys, one of whom went to Harrow County School from 1926 to 1929. Then in 1914 he was made a district official of the union. His work in this role found him towards the left wing of the political spectrum, but he gradually moved to the right as he grew older and as he progressed up the leadership ladder.

By 1925 he was at the Trades Union Congress as assistant secretary when – as the old cliché has it – 'fate stepped in'. The general secretary was Fred Bramley, himself only two years in the post. While he was attending an international trade union meeting in Amsterdam in November 1925 he collapsed and died, leaving Citrine as acting general secretary.

The twenties were a turbulent era in the industrial world in this country, with the miners continually pressing their case for improvements in their terrible underground conditions, and other unions notably the railwaymen stood by them in a period of severe unemployment and growing tension between employers and workers. The stage was set for what became Britain's only general strike. Citrine, as acting general secretary (he was not confirmed in the post until later that year) was thrust into the centre of the stage of this massive, but ill-fated, conflict. There still continue to be arguments about the conduct of the strike both from the government side and that of the trade unions. When the strike was called off after ten days, the miners blamed the General Council of the TUC for not giving them enough support. Citrine was at the centre of it and he wrote after the event:

> I do not regard the General Strike as a failure [...] It was never aimed against the state as a challenge to the Constitution. It was a protest against the degradation of the standards of life of millions of good trade unionists. It was a sympathetic strike on a national scale.

(Quoted by Margaret Morris in her book, *The General Strike*.)

He and his family came to live in Wembley, at 63 Kingsway – near King Edward's Park – from which he eventually derived his peerage title. Having attained the highest rank in the trade union movement at an unexpectedly early age, he set out to transform the 'carthorse' as David Low the cartoonist saw it. The fact that he did not fully succeed must be blamed on the inherently cautious (I hesitate to term it 'conservative') attitude of some top-ranking unionists. He was sufficiently recognised as a driving force by his knighthood in 1935. He and Bevin demanded recognition of the right of the trade union movement to be consulted by government on matters concerning workers' rights and conditions. He had a genius for organisation and rationalised the TUC office; together with Bevin, he promoted the expansion of workers' education especially through links with Ruskin College Oxford.

His position became more strongly a supporter of the Labour Party under Lansbury and then Attlee – and he had opposed Ramsay McDonald. He was just as strongly opposed to the influence of the Communist Party in trade union affairs - and kept up a constant battle, particularly with Harry Pollitt its then general secretary.

In his role as leader of the TUC, he was a great traveller, going to the International Federation (of which he was president from 1928 to 1945); to Russia to see for himself the working of the Soviet experiment; to Finland and to America – all of which he recorded in books recounting his visits. He was untiring in his work for the TUC as he was in his journeying abroad.

For the same reasons that he had opposed Ramsay McDonald and Philip Snowden, he welcomed Clement Attlee when he became Prime Minister in 1945. This was mainly because he saw him as a leader who was truly in support of the Labour Party, working for nationalisation and for the improvement of working people. When he retired from the TUC after twenty years – the longest serving general secretary – he demonstrated the view that trade unionists should play their part in the conduct of industry by becoming a member of the new National Coal Board and then the first chairman of the Central Electricity Board in 1947 (the time he was made a peer), and saw it through its first ten years.

Walter Citrine – the elder statesman of the Trade Union Movement. (Courtesy Trades Union Congress)

He continued to serve industry on a part-time basis for several years more and then retired. His wife, Doris died in 1973; he went to live in Devon and died in 1983 at the grand age of ninety-six.

John Kelly – Teacher of Renown

John Kelly was born in 1874 and after training to be a teacher he came to Willesden, where he taught for forty-four years, thirty of these as a head teacher, until his retirement in 1934. He was also a committed trade unionist and, as a member of the National Union of Teachers, he was a Willesden Branch delegate at thirty-six or more Annual Conferences – which must be something of a record. He was a teacher representative on the Willesden Education Committee in 1905 and subsequent years.

In 1904, a the young age of thirty, he became head of Dudden Hill (Boys') School; a post he held, with increasing respect for his achievements until he retired in February 1934 at the age of sixty.

At his retirement reception, held at the school the following week, a large gathering came to pay tribute to someone who had earned 'the deepest gratitude of hundreds of scholars and had won the firmest respect of all the members of staff who worked under him' as *The Willesden Chronicle* reported. The chair would have been taken by Alderman William Hill, the chairman of the Willesden Education Committee, but in his absence, the Director of Education, the renowned Dr Evan Davies, took over.

The tributes were, rightly, fulsome and came from the National Secretary of the NUT (Mr Fred Mander), from John Wilmot MP for East Fulham at that time (a nephew of Mr Kelly and later a Labour Minister), from staff, old boys and his local Union Branch, the Willesden

Mr John Kelly. (Courtesy John Kelly Boys' Technology College)

John Kelly Boys' High School.

Teachers' Association. With him at this memorable occasion, as it must have been for all who were there, were his wife, who he described as a 'wonderful help-meet' and his son H.J. Kelly and daughters 'Miss M. and E. Kelly'.

Having retired, he used his talents and experience in the service of the community by becoming a Labour County Councillor of the Middlesex County Council, representing Church End Division from 1934 to 1946.

Ray Dore-Boize (a long serving whip for the Willesden and Brent Labour Groups) was a pupil at the school when Mr Kelly was head and remembers him as a very good head and a Christian Socialist. In the 1920s he campaigned for the local MP with the cry, 'vote, vote, vote for

Sammy Viant'! He met him again during the war when Ray was in the army in Northampton and Mr Kelly, now in his early seventies, was helping the evacuees from Willesden. And, from there, he would travel down to London twice a week to attend meetings of the Middlesex County Council!

He died in May 1955 at the age of eighty-one and, later, the Willesden Education Committee decided to name the new schools for Boys and Girls on Dollis Hill in his honour. The schools prospered, especially as, under Brent (after Kilburn Grammar and Brondesbury and Kilburn Schools had merged) they remained only the single-sex non-denominational high schools in the borough. With long-serving head teachers (following their namesake's example perhaps) they took up the challenge of technology colleges with reputations which John Kelly himself would have welcomed.

Index